The Freudian Reading

The Freudian Reading

Analytical and Fictional Constructions

Lis Møller

upp

UNIVERSITY OF PENNSYLVANIA PRESS   Philadelphia

Permission to reprint published material is acknowledged:
From *The Standard Edition of the Complete Psychological Works of Sigmund Freud*, translated
and edited by James Strachey in collaboration with Anna Freud, and assisted by Alix
Strachey and Alan Tyson. Copyright © 1953–1974 by Sigmund Freud Copyrights, the
Institute of Psycho-Analysis, and Hogarth Press. Reprinted by permission of Random
Century Group (world rights); selected essays are reprinted with permission of Basic
Books, Inc., and Unwin Hyman (U.S. rights).

From *Narrative Truth and Historical Truth: Meaning and Interpretation in Psychoanalysis*, by
Donald P. Spence. New York and London: W.W. Norton and Company, 1982.
Copyright © 1982 by Donald P. Spence. Reprinted by permission of Donald P.
Spence.

Library of Congress Cataloging-in-Publication Data
Møller, Lis.
  The Freudian reading: analytical and fictional constructions / Lis Møller.
    p. cm.
  Includes bibliographical references and index.
  ISBN 0-8122-3126-0 (cloth). — ISBN 0-8122-1381-5 (paper)
  1. Freud, Sigmund, 1856–1939.   2. Psychological literature.
3. Psychoanalysis and literature.   4. Hermeneutics—History—20th century. I. Title.
BF109.F74M65   1991
150.19′52—dc20   91-22539
                                                                   CIP

To the memory of
Anne Marie Rahbæk Møller

Contents

Preface

As Philip Rieff has said, the originality of psychoanalysis "lies chiefly in its hermeneutic skills."[1] Freud set out to found a "scientific psychology," but found instead an immensely powerful interpretive method that reaches out to embrace all kinds of semiotic practice, from hysterical symptoms, dreams, and parapraxes to religious systems, art, and literature.

The present study is a critical exposition of psychoanalytic strategies of reading and of Freudian hermeneutics, with special reference to the ways in which this hermeneutics has informed, and is informed by, literary studies. It takes its point of departure in the question: What is involved in a psychoanalytic interpretation (of a literary text)? As indicated by the enormous body of recent works dealing with psychoanalysis and the possible conjunctions between psychoanalysis and literature, psychoanalytic interpretation is still a highly controverted field of inquiry. What *is,* in fact, a "Freudian reading"? In the following I shall approach this question through another question: What kind of a reader was Freud? A recent study describes Freud's endeavor as a quest for coherent and exhaustive explanation, motivated by the assumption that "all human thought and behavior had a meaning and meanings—that they were understandable, purposeful, had structure and rose to significance."[2] Not surprisingly, Freud has been called the "great synthesizer." His ability to make sense out of nonsense, to comprehend the significance of that which appears to be purely random or marginal, and to link together seemingly unrelated events continues to baffle his readers. And yet the opinion that underlies my study is that Freud's power as a reader shows itself not so much in his capacity for persuasive synthesis as in his will to press his inquiry to the point where he encounters the unreadable—that which he *cannot* explain; that which does not fit in with his explanatory system; or that which he can only explain at the risk of overthrowing previous conclusions. Such moments of crisis, which one encounters everywhere in Freud's writings, are highly significant points of rupture: problems he believed he had solved suddenly present themselves in a new and disturbing light, causing him to swerve from his original train of thought, or even to call in question the theoretical foundation of his interpretation. Coherence, comprehensiveness, and closure may be what the analyst aims at; it is, however, rarely what we get—and this may be the reason why we keep coming back to Freud's text, not just to consult it, but to *read* it.

The following is an inquiry into Freudian hermeneutics that proceeds by means of a close reading of Freud's own readings, with special attention given to the shifts and turns of his argument.[3] I divide my inquiry into two distinct sections. I begin with the case stories and the papers on technique, and go on to discuss psychoanalytic literary analysis. Yet, in each case, my topic is the nature of the interpretive process rather than the contents of the particular interpretation, and the questions that I wish to raise are the same: What are the premises, procedures, and objectives of the psychoanalytic reading? What kind of knowledge (or "truth") does it produce? What is the analyst in search of? How should we conceive of the relationship between his object of investigation and the interpretative discourse of psychoanalysis? Taking as my point of departure that which I have called "moments of crisis" in Freud's argument, I show that he has no final answer to these questions. Freud's work does not present a uniform theory of interpretation, which would provide for a coherent account of the object, procedure, purpose, and epistemological status of the psychoanalytic interpretation. His work, I argue, is the scene of the encounter of different, conflicting, and even incompatible theories of reading. The dominant line of argument is punctuated with problems and questions, leading to revisions that compel us to reconsider our idea of a "Freudian reading."

The Freudian Reading considers a wide selection of Freud's writings, from *Studies on Hysteria* (1893–95) to *Moses and Monotheism* (1939), but special attention is given to four texts: *Delusions and Dreams in Jensen's Gradiva* (1907), *From the History of an Infantile Neurosis* (1918), "The Uncanny" (1919), and "Constructions in Analysis" (1937). Rather than adopting a chronological approach, I explore the ways in which these four texts interact: how they reflect, contradict, comment on, and illuminate each other. This interaction is the structuring principle of my study, which is divided into three parts. Part 1, "Reconstruction/ Construction," deals mainly with "Constructions in Analysis," leading up to Part 2, "Stories of Reading," which pits *Delusions and Dreams* against *From the History of an Infantile Neurosis*. In Part 3, "Psychoanalysis and Literature," I return to Freud's interpretation of *Gradiva* in order to read "The Uncanny" in light of *Delusions and Dreams*.

From "Constructions in Analysis" I draw the concept of construction (or *re*construction), which is one of the key terms of my study. The notion of (re)construction provides me with a connecting link between the psychoanalyst's "reading" of his patient and his reading of a literary text. In order to create a coherent account of his patient's "forgotten years," the analyst must rearrange and fill in gaps in the material the analysand produces in the course of the treatment. Analysis is shown to revolve around a void—a hole in the analysand's memory that can only be filled by the analyst's construction. However, reconstruction is also Freud's term for psychoanalytic literary analysis. The analyst, he says, must "reconstruct" the "original arrangement" of the textual "elements."[4] Most importantly, however, the term (re)construction is itself suspended between different understandings of psychoanalytic interpretation in Freud's work.

(Re)construction is associated with the archaeological metaphor that is so prominent in Freudian hermeneutics. The analytical construction is represented as a counterpart to reconstruction in the field of archaeology, which, in Malcolm Bowie's words, "provided Freud with a promise of completeness and adequacy in his own scientific explanations."[5]

Construction is also the mark of the fictionality of psychoanalytic interpretation. The analytical construction belongs within the realm of "as if" or "as though." It is a hypothesis, suggested by the analyst, that occupies an empty space in the patient's narrative about the past, but which is verifiable only in the present. How should we, then, conceive of the analyst's work of construction? Does analysis produce narratives "from" the analysand's past, or rather narratives "relating to"[6] the past? Does meaning emerge from the fragments of memory unearthed in the course of the analytical process, or is meaning conferred upon these fragments in the dialogical space of psychoanalytic therapy? "Constructions in Analysis" provides no definitive answer, but oscillates between different conceptions of the psychoanalytic process, between different epistemological models. To explore in greater detail these divergent lines of argument is the aim of Part 2, in which I juxtapose *Delusions and Dreams in Jensen's* Gradiva and *From the History of an Infantile Neurosis* in order to outline two distinct "stories of reading" in Freud's work—that is, two different accounts of the procedures and the objectives of psychoanalytic interpretation.

Freud used several analogies and metaphors in order to account for reading in psychoanalysis, but none of these has proved more pervasive than the archaeological metaphor, which appears to be inex-

tricably bound up with the very idea of psychoanalysis as a *depth* hermeneutics. In Chapter 2 I examine in detail this figure, taking as my main
example Wilhelm Jensen's novel, *Gradiva: A Pompeian Phantasy*, which,
in Freud's reading, is brought to dramatize the analogy between, on the
one hand, repression and the burial of Pompeii and, on the other
hand, the psychoanalytic process and the archaeologist's work of excavation and reconstruction. In psychoanalytic thinking, *Gradiva*, I
shall argue, becomes the emblematic story of psychoanalysis as an
archaeology of the soul. But as "excavation" and "reconstruction" in
Jensen's novel take the form of an unpacking of a language Freud
describes as "poetical," this story of reading may be extended to the
field of literary criticism. In Chapter 4, I return to *Delusions and Dreams
in Jensen's* Gradiva, in order to examine, in the light of the analogy between psychoanalysis and archaeology, Freud's idea of a psychoanalytic
literary criticism, as well as his own interpretation of Jensen's novel.

Recently, the American psychoanalyst Donald P. Spence has asserted that psychoanalysis needs new metaphors. Taking vigorous ex-
ception to Freud's analogy with archaeology, Spence suggests that we
should start looking for a possible alternative, for "we will never step
out from under the reigning metaphor unless we have a metaphor to
take its place."[7] But as Lacan[8] and Derrida's bold re-readings of Freud's
work have shown, significant alternatives to the archaeological metaphor and to the idea of the past as a buried Pompeii have, in fact, been
present from the onset. In a draft from 1896 Freud advances the thesis
that memory-traces from time to time are subjected to a rearrangement
or a *"re-transcription"*[9] in accordance with fresh circumstances. In the
papers from the nineties, Freud turns to such textual metaphors in
order to account for the otherwise inexplicable temporal gap between,
on the one hand, the event that allegedly constitutes the trauma and,
on the other hand, the pathological response to the traumatic incident,
the outbreak of a neurosis. Memories, he claims, are retranscribed in
accordance with subsequent impressions; retroactively they acquire a
new meaning that allows them to operate in the present *"as though they
were fresh experiences."*[10] "Re-transcription," then, pertains to the mechanism designated, in *From the History of an Infantile Neurosis*, by the term
"deferred action" (*Nacträglichkeit*). Chapter 3 discusses this important
concept, which challenges the idea of the unconscious (the repressed)
as a buried Pompeii. What most concerns me, however, are the ways in
which Freud, in the case of the Wolf Man, brings the logic of deferred
action to bear on his idea of construction in analysis, thus locating the
psychoanalytic reading at the point of intersection of a dialogical and a
temporal axis. *From the History of an Infantile Neurosis*, therefore, pre-

sents us with a story of reading that constitutes a viable alternative to the archaeological story of excavation and reconstruction.

Peter Brooks, in a recently published essay, has declared that psychoanalytic literary criticism is something of an embarrassment that mostly deserves the bad name it has made for itself.[11] But does Freud's work—his readings of fictional texts, his attempts to arrive at a psychoanalytic theory of literature and creativity—in fact authorize the kind of criticism evoked by the term psychoanalytic literary criticism? Indeed, his literary interpretations certainly lay the foundations for the kind of criticism Brooks and others reject. Consequently, it has been argued that "Freud's principal literary speculation is not to be found in the familiar psychosexual reductions that tend to characterize his own overt attempt at the psychoanalysis of art."[12] However, as I shall argue in Part 3, such a characterization overlooks the fact that Freud's own readings of literary texts invariably transcend the "reductions" commonly associated with traditional psychoanalytic criticism. Freud never contents himself merely with posing those questions to which he has the answers; he also poses problems to which he has no solution, or which he can only solve by revising the theoretical foundation of his reading. As a consequence, his interpretations of literary works may seem strangely unfulfilled. In this, I shall argue, is their primary strength. Taking as my main examples *Delusions and Dreams in Jensen's Gradiva* and Freud's analysis of E. T. A. Hoffmann's "The Sandman" in "The Uncanny," I show that these readings present the same pattern: in each case a dogmatic and highly authoritarian psychoanalytic interpretation is undermined from within, as it encounters the unreadable.

"Dächte die Psychoanalyse ihr Prinzip zu Ende," writes Theodor W. Adorno, "so müsste sie . . . die Abschaffung der Kunst verlangen, die sie ohnehin in ihren Patienten weganalysieren geneigt ist."[13] Such an abolition of art (fictionality) seems indeed to be the consequence of Freud's reading of *Gradiva,* for the purpose of this interpretation is to show that the novel is a "perfectly correct psychiatric study"—a psychiatric study that has merely disguised itself as a "Phantasy."[14] Ironically, this interpretation runs up against a textual element it cannot explain, and which momentarily throws it off balance. This textual element is the highly "improbable premiss" on which the entire story depends, the very mark of its fictionality. In his attempt to cope with this alogical element, which frustrates his total explanatory ambitions, Freud launches an interpretative hypothesis that unsettles not only his psychoanalytic reading of the novel but also the story of reading the novel supposedly dramatizes. In the "Oedipal" reading of "The Sandman" in "The Uncanny" (which I discuss in Chapter 5) I find a very similar structure. In "The Uncanny," however, the unreadable is allowed to enter Freud's argument, causing him to revise his theory of the uncanny, as well as his idea of a "Freudian reading."

I began working on this book in 1985–86, during a stay at Yale University made possible by generous grants from the Fulbright Commission and the Denmark America Foundation as well as from the Danish Research Council for the Humanities, who also supported a final revision of the manuscript. I am most grateful to faculty and students in the departments of Comparative Literature and English at Yale who created a stimulating and challenging environment that has played a major role in the formation of this book. I wish to express my thanks as well to those who read preliminary versions of parts of my manuscript, in particular Geoffrey H. Hartman and J. Hillis Miller, and to my friends Gery Bruederlin, Helle Porsdam, Bryan Short, and Yoshiko Tomishima. My greatest debt of gratitude, however, is to Peter Brooks, whose work in the field of psychoanalysis and literature has been a major source of inspiration and who kindly read more than one version of *The Freudian Reading*. I also wish to express my thanks to my colleagues and my students at the University of Copenhagen and to colleagues in Denmark and Norway with whom I have discussed aspects of this work; to the staff of the Freud Museum in London; and to the two anonymous readers at University of Pennsylvania Press, whose criticism and suggestions have been most helpful. Finally, I want to thank my parents—and my husband Søren for his patience and support during the process of writing and rewriting this book.

Part One
Reconstruction/Construction

Chapter 1

The Analytical Construction: Psychoanalysis and Truth

Toward the end of *Leonardo da Vinci and a Memory of His Childhood,* Freud pauses to reflect on the contribution of psychoanalysis to the field of biography in general, and on his own psychobiographic study of the work of Leonardo in particular. Maybe, Freud remarks, this study will provoke "the criticism, even from friends of psycho-analysis and from those who are expert in it, that I have merely written a psycho-analytic novel."[1] The notion of a "psycho-analytic novel" sounds familiar. Not only does the critique Freud anticipates echo the condescending comment to one of his first papers: it sounds "like a scientific fairy tale."[2] Freud himself has, albeit in a different context, referred to psychoanalytic case stories in similar terms. It "strikes me myself as strange," he says in *Studies on Hysteria,* "that the case histories I write should read like short stories and that, as one might say, they lack the serious stamp of science."[3] In *Leonardo da Vinci and a Memory of His Childhood,* the predicate "psycho-analytic novel" pertains to the question of the "certainty" or the "truth" (p. 134) of the results this reading has produced, that is, the content of the interpretation. In *Studies on Hysteria,* the emphasis is on the dependence of psychoanalysis on narrative as a form of representation and as explanatory structure. It may be, however, that the question of truth, of the epistemological status of psychoanalytic readings, is inextricably bound up with the issue of the role of narrative and narrative structures in psychoanalysis. This, at least, is the point Donald P. Spence wishes to make in *Narrative Truth and Historical Truth: Meaning and Interpretation in Psychoanalysis.*[4]

Narrative Truth and Historical Truth begins by drawing attention to the impact on psychoanalysis of what Spence calls "narrative tradition." Freud's case stories, he says, have "made us aware of the persuasive power of a coherent narrative—in particular, of the way in which an aptly chosen reconstruction can fill the gap between two apparently unrelated events and, in the process, make sense out of nonsense" (p. 21). As reader and analyst, Freud was always in search of the underlying thread or the hidden pattern of what his patients told him. According to Spence, the demand for sequence, continuity, and connection has become the guiding principle of psychoanalytic therapy; in fact, reading in psychoanalysis is reading with a view to narrative coherence. But narrative coherence is at the same time seen as evidence of the correctness of the analysis or as a sign of truth; indeed, the very consistency of an interpretation or a case story led Freud to believe that he was "making contact with an actual happening" (p. 27). The tradition within which Freud was working did not allow him to distinguish between, on the one hand, the account that makes sense of seemingly discontinuous and disjunctive material and, on the other hand, the patient's actual history. The outcome of this is not merely a confusion of ideas in psychoanalysis. Freud's failure to distinguish between convincing explanations and "things as they actually were" prevented him from understanding that the uncovering of an actual past may be of far less importance to psychoanalytic therapy than the creation of a coherent account that synthesizes a particular set of events. A well-constructed narrative has a special significance in its own right. It even possesses a kind of truth, a "truth that is real and immediate and carries an important significance for the process of therapeutic change" (p. 21).

In psychoanalysis, the German psychoanalyst Wolfgang Loch argues, "we are confronted with two notions of truth: Truth understood as the correct statement, the historical fact—only in need of discovery to be brought to the surface; and truth as the emergent, the construction of something that makes sense and therefore permits one to rely on it and to continue living."[5] In order to dissociate the notion of an account of things as they actually were from the notion of a therapeutically effective story that has been constructed in the course of the analytical process, Spence, too, adopts the idea of two different concepts of truth in psychoanalysis. He proposes a distinction between "historical truth" and "narrative truth," defining the latter as "the criterion we use to decide when a certain experience has been captured to our satisfaction; it depends on continuity and closure and the extent to which the fit of the pieces takes on an aesthetic finality" (p. 31). Roughly, "narrative truth" designates the kind of truth psychoanalysis may in fact produce; "historical truth," on the other hand, is based in Freud's conception of psychoanalytic epistemology and is closely associated with his self-image as archaeologist.

As Spence remarks, Freud was fond of representing himself as a kind of archaeologist, "uncovering pieces of the past" (p. 27). In so doing, he misconstrued the psychoanalytical process, confused the construction of a well-organized narrative, "narrative truth," with the excavation of a past reality, and prevented himself from seeing that cure does not depend on the recuperation of a historical truth. The curative interpretation is the persuasive interpretation—and interpretations are persuasive not because of their "evidential value" but because of their "rhetorical appeal" (p. 32). As an alternative to Freud's archaeological model of psychoanalysis, Spence therefore offers an "artistic" model (p. 270). "It may be useful," he says, "to think of an interpretation as being a certain kind of aesthetic experience as opposed to being an utterance that is either (historically) true or false" (p. 268).

Spence's discussion of the psychoanalytic process prompts a number of crucial questions: What kind of reality do psychoanalytic interpretations bring to light? What kind of truth value do they possess? How should we conceive of the relationship between the patient's past life and the analytical reconstruction of this life? What kinds of explanatory models and structures are applied to the material produced in the course of the psychoanalytical process? To what extent do these models govern the analytical process? What is, in fact, a "psychoanalytic interpretation"? By substituting narrative truth for historical truth, Spence has indeed challenged preconceived ideas of psychoanalytic epistemology. I find, however, that his conceptual framework, his definitions of narrative and historical truth, and the critique of Freudianism that his study articulates are problematic as well as suggestive. In rereading Freud in the light of *Narrative Truth and Historical Truth,* one discovers not the blind, unwitting confusion of two notions of truth that Spence has postulated, but rather the fundamental heterogeneity of Freud's argument.

While on the one hand polemically asserting the authenticity of the analytical findings, Freud, on the other hand, clearly acknowledges the problems to which Spence calls attention, and in his discussions of psychoanalytic epistemology he not only anticipates Spence's idea of narrative truth, but goes beyond the vague and insufficient definition of narrative truth as "a good story" (p. 31). Thus Freud's account of the psychoanalytic process and his discussion of the validity of psychoanalytic interpretations and constructions is less simple and less unequivocal than Spence is prepared to admit. This, too, applies to the notion of historical truth, a Freudian term that Spence has domesticated by lifting it out of its context. If Spence's critique of psychoanalysis invites us to reread Freud, this critical rereading, in turn, allows us to problematize Spence's use of the term historical truth in opposition to narrative truth.

Later in this chapter I return to Freud's concept of historical truth, but before I proceed to a discussion of the psychoanalytic process, let me turn to a somewhat different field of inquiry, namely psychoanalytic literary criticism. For it seems that Spence's distinction between historical and narrative truth, problematic as these terms may be, can provide us with an approach to the discussion of the possible conjunctions between psychoanalysis and literature, or between psychoanalysis and literary criticism. Though Spence's study does not deal with questions of the interpretation of literary works, his characterization of Freudian epistemology may, I think, be extended to the field of traditional psychoanalytic literary criticism.[6] I perceive an affinity, in some respects, between, on the one hand, Spence's revaluation of psychoanalytic truth and, on the other hand, recent attempts on the part of literary critics and theorists to redefine the relationship between psychoanalysis and literary study. However, I also intend to show how the contributions of these critics and theorists may in turn query Spence's critique of Freud in general, and his "aesthetic" model of psychoanalysis in particular.

"The poets and philosophers before me discovered the unconscious," remarked Freud when he, at his seventieth birthday, was celebrated as the discoverer of the unconscious. "What I discovered was the scientific method by which the unconscious can be studied."[7] This often-quoted observation sums up the traditional conception of the affinity, as well as the fundamental difference, between psychoanalysis and literature. The field of study of psychoanalysis, "the human mind," is indeed, writes Freud, the "domain" most the creative writer's own. Thus psychoanalysis and literature draw from the same source and explore "the same object."[8] But, as he goes on to say, they explore it differently. The unconscious that is embodied in the literary text becomes, in psychoanalysis, the object of a systematic, if not scientific, investigation.

Freud's definition of the affinities and differences between psychoanalysis and literature articulates the ideas that form the basis of traditional psychoanalytic literary criticism—whether it perceives its object of inquiry as being literature as mise-en-scène of unconscious fantasies, the literary text as expression and artistic elaboration of its author's repressed wishes, or literature as that which allows the reader to enjoy his own fantasies and rework his own psychic conflicts. This definition, furthermore, explains the attraction that psychoanalysis has had, and still has, for literary critics. First of all, psychoanalysis claims to have investigated those aspects of human life that form the subject matter of literature, and seems moreover to provide an interpretive method that opens up new perspectives in literary studies. Thus psychoanalytic critics from Ernest Jones onward have carefully pointed out how psychoanalytic interpretation explains those dimensions of the literary work other interpretations cannot account for. Psychoanalysis appears to offer a method for penetrating "the deepest levels of meaning,"[9] for revealing, exploring, and explaining the innermost dynamics of the literary text, and for uncovering those vital sources of inspiration that remain inaccessible even to the author.

Secondly, psychoanalysis, while having defined its object of inquiry as being the "domain" that "indeed" is the domain of literature, nevertheless holds the promise of an interpretive position safely outside literature, that is to say, free of the uncertainties and ambiguities that characterize the field of literary studies. Psychoanalytic theory—understood as a "systematic and well-validated body of knowledge" about the "forces" with which "the greatest writers of fiction have been preoccupied"[10]—seems to provide literary analysis with something like a scientific foundation. This, at least, is the function psychoanalysis appears to perform for traditional psychoanalytic critics. From the point of view of these critics, psychoanalysis occupies the position of an "effectively secured" discipline, of a field of study that is "effectively free of the kind of epistemological and methodological disputes that agitate their own areas of inquiry."[11] Psychoanalytic theory, claims C. Barry Chabot, secures the analyst's interpretive activities in a way literary critics must envy.[12]

But if Freud's understanding of the relationship between psychoanalysis and literature accounts for the allurements of psychoanalysis, this understanding, by the same token, explains the discontents of psychoanalytic literary criticism. Allegations of reductionism have from the beginning attended the psychoanalytic critic's attempt to uncover the deepest levels of meaning. The record of the Freudian critical tradition "all too clearly shows that a special danger of dogmatism, of clinical presumption, indeed of monomania, accompanies a method that purports to ferret out from literature a handful of previously known, perennially 'deep' psychic concerns," writes Frederick Crews toward the end of *Out of My System,* a study that documents the author's growing dissatisfaction with the methods he himself has applied to the study of literature.[13] Psychoanalysis, claims a more recent work, is "a discourse of mastery."[14] That which is usually understood by the term psychoanalytic criticism invariably entails the submission of literature to the supreme authority of psychoanalytic theory. "While literature is considered as a body of *language*—to *be interpreted*—psychoanalysis is considered as a body of *knowledge,* whose competence is called upon *to interpret.*"[15] Such a ranking of discourses seems, indeed, inherent in Freud's understanding of literature. As long as literature is defined primarily in (depth) psychological terms, as "description of the human mind," or even as poetical elaboration of unconscious mental material that "has to be extensively transformed and purified before it can be presented to consciousness,"[16] the literary work will remain dependent on the insights and the explanatory power of the psychoanalyst, who restates in scientific language what the poet could only express in distorted form.

However, as several critics have pointed out, the crucial question remains whether Freud (i.e., Freud's text) in fact authorizes the kind of psychoanalytic literary criticism he himself initiated. Indeed, this is one of the questions around which the present study revolves. Let me here say that he does and yet does not, and that the very ambiguity of my answer is suggestive of that which is so fundamentally problematic about traditional psychoanalytic criticism. Psychoanalytic critics have always been accused by their adversaries of being poor readers of literature. This is not necessarily true. The problem lies elsewhere: these critics have, almost of necessity, been poor readers of Freud. Taking as their point of departure the idea of psychoanalysis as a "well-validated" body of knowledge, they have been unable to go beyond the "canonical" reception of Freud. Psychoanalytic critics have read *through* Freud, but failed to *read* Freud's text. This last point prompts a return to *Narrative Truth and Historical Truth,* since Spence's study has raised some of the crucial questions psychoanalytic critics have refrained from asking.

First of all, Spence has queried the very authority of psychoanalytic interpretation by refusing to grant the psychoanalytic construction of the past the status of an account that is historically true. Or rather, he has raised the question: What kind of interpretive authority does psychoanalysis possess? Now, the authority of psychoanalysis is precisely what is taken for granted by traditional psychoanalytic criticism. In fact, we may say that the basic premise of psychoanalytic criticism is the belief that psychoanalysis indeed uncovers what Spence has called a historical truth. While recognizing the difference between patient and literary text and between therapeutic process and literary analysis, psychoanalytic criticism nevertheless derives its methodology, its objectives, and, as it were, its authority from the psychoanalytic process, from the psychoanalyst's reading of his patient. In this respect, Spence's calling into question of the assumption that the psychoanalytic interpretation brings to light a reality or a truth existing prior to and independent of the analytical process has an immediate bearing on psychoanalytic criticism. If, as André Green maintains, the psychoanalyst "constructs a meaning which has never been created before the analytic relationship began,"[17] rather than simply unveiling a hidden meaning, what, then, is the epistemological status of the unconscious content that the psychoanalytic critic brings to light? The authority of psychoanalytic interpretation of literature depends on the assumption that the literary text conceals and yet reveals a latent content that psychoanalysis has the power to demask and reconstruct (restore); it depends on the assumption that the task of the critic is to reveal hidden layers of meaning, to bring to light the latent truth. If psychoanalysis is not, or cannot be, an "archaeological excavation" and reconstruction of a buried content, what, then, is the raison d'être of psychoanalytic criticism?

What is at stake in Spence's critique of Freud's conception of the psychoanalytic process in general and his archaeological metaphor in particular is, in fact, the surface/depth paradigm in psychoanalysis, or to be more specific, the idea of psychoanalysis as a *depth* psychology or a *depth* hermeneutics that sets "aside the surface meaning in favor of the latent intent" or sees "the surface meaning as a derivate of some piece of the patient's unconscious."[18] The surface/depth paradigm has from the very beginning informed the psychoanalytic critic's concept of literature and textuality. Archaeological and geological metaphors appear in abundance in traditional studies such as Lesser's *Fiction and the Unconscious,* which habitually refers to "buried levels of meaning" (p. 205). A story, says Simon Lesser, "has many different meanings, layer upon layer of significance. . . . In fact, topographically one would have to picture the various meanings of which an overdetermined work admits as extending not outward in space, but downward or inward" (pp. 113–14). And, as later contributions show, these spatial metaphors have been surprisingly persistent.[19] It is true that many traditional psychoanalytic critics have pointed out that more attention should be given to the textual surface, that is, the obvious meaning and the form of the literary work. They have not, however, queried the adequacy of the surface/depth model itself. This is where Spence's critique enters into the picture—and seems to join forces with recent attempts, on the part of literary critics and theorists, to reinvent the relationship between psychoanalysis and literature.

Shoshana Felman, no doubt the most prominent critic of traditional applied psychoanalysis,[20] is one of the theorists who have contested the surface/depth paradigm. In "On Reading Poetry: Reflections on the Limits and Possibilities of Psychoanalytic Approaches," which pits Lacan's reading of Poe's "Purloined Letter" against Marie Bonaparte's classic psycho-biographic study, she presents Lacan's analysis of the signifier as "a radical reversal of the traditional expectations and presuppositions involved in the common psychoanalytic approach to literature, and its invariable search for hidden meanings." Unlike Bonaparte, who sees the analyst's task as the uncovering of a content "*hidden* somewhere in the real, in some secret biographical *depth*," Lacan "makes the principle of symbolic evidence the guideline for an analysis not of the signified but of the signifier—for an analysis of the unconscious (the repressed) not as hidden, but on the contrary as *exposed*—in language—through significant (rhetorical) displacement."[21] We can thus establish a certain affinity between Spence's critique of the archaeological metaphor in psychoanalysis and Felman's critique of the traditional psychoanalytic critic's search for hidden meanings. However, this comparison reveals at the same time a fundamental difference that, I think, shows the limitations of Spence's enterprise. While Felman's deconstruction of the surface/depth model in psychoanalytic criticism is made possible by Lacan's rereading of the Freudian unconscious, Spence's project tends to dismiss altogether the concept of the unconscious, a term that remains almost synonymous with psychoanalysis itself.[22]

As regards Spence's concept of narrative truth and its connection with recent discussions of psychoanalysis and literature, one finds a similar relationship of consent and dissent. By calling attention to Freud's dependence on a narrative tradition and by introducing the concept of narrative truth, Spence invites us to reconsider the relationship between psychoanalysis and literary studies. Of course, his study does not explicitly deal with this issue. *Narrative Truth and Historical Truth* is written by a psychoanalyst and addressed primarily, so it seems, to other psychoanalysts. But from the perspective of literary criticism and theory, this is in fact one of the appealing features of Spence's book. Ever since the birth of psychoanalysis, psychoanalysts as well as literary critics have used psychoanalytic theory to explain literature. Here we have the opposite: a psychoanalyst who finds that he has to turn to literature and to literary theory, or more precisely narrative theory, in order to describe the psychoanalytic process and to understand psychoanalytic explanatory models. Spence's conception of psychoanalytic interpretation as a "certain kind of aesthetic experience" suggests that the relationship between psychoanalysis and literature is less unequivocal than traditional psychoanalytic criticism has tended to assume. Psychoanalysis, it is maintained, cannot dispense with narratives and narrative structures. Psychoanalytic theory, writes Roy Schafer, whose work inspired Spence's study, may be seen as a set of "codes" or "narrative structures" employed in order to "generate psychoanalytic meaning."[23] From the point of view of Spence and Schafer, then, psychoanalysis involves what may be described as *literary* problems. After all, it is implied, psychoanalysis is not effectively free of the epistemological and methodological disputes that agitate the field of literary studies.

While the basic premise of traditional psychoanalytic criticism is indeed the idea of a clear distinction between psychoanalysis and literature, a distinction that enables psychoanalysis to assume the status of an external grounding text, the recognition that psychoanalysis and literature "implicate each other"[24] has in recent years renewed the discussion of the possible conjunctions of psychoanalysis with literary studies. This recent development marks a shift of emphasis: from the position that psychoanalysis explains literature and secures literary analysis, because literature is basically a "psychological" phenomenon, to the position that Freud's text is of relevance to literary criticism and theory, because psychoanalytic interpretation implicitly as well as explicitly deals with questions of literature.

The recognition that psychoanalysis is not safely outside literature, which would seem to call into question the very possibility of a psychoanalytic literary criticism, has in fact opened up a new and heterogeneous field of study even as it has motivated a rereading of Freud's text by literary critics and theorists. Within this new field of study, the study of narrative and of "the narrativity of the structure of explanation"[25] has proved particularly fruitful. While some critics have explored the literary qualities of Freud's case stories, others, most notably Peter Brooks, have argued that psychoanalysis is "implicitly a narratology."[26] If there seems at first sight, however, to be an obvious affinity between Spence's study and the work of the critics and theorists who concern themselves with psychoanalysis and narrativity, it is, at the same time, the close readings, by these critics and theorists, of Freud's text that allow us to problematize not only Spence's definition of narrative truth, but also his too facile critique, which ignores the complexity of Freud's argument.

As we have already seen, Freud was himself aware of the dependence of psychoanalysis on narrative structures, as well as of the "narrativizing at the very heart of the psychoanalytic process."[27] In one of his early case stories, *Fragment of an Analysis of a Case of Hysteria* (1905), better known as the case of Dora, Freud has explicitly described the psychoanalytic process in narrational terms. It is therefore no coincidence that precisely this case story has lately received so much attention from literary critics.[28] Reflecting on the difficulty of beginning his account of the case—indeed, on the difficulty of reporting a case—Freud remarks that he cannot help wondering why others can provide such "smooth and precise histories in cases of hysteria."[29] As a matter of fact, the patients themselves are incapable of giving such reports of the history of their lives. "I begin the treatment," writes Freud, "by asking the patient to give me the whole story of his life and illness, but even so the information I receive is never enough to let me see my way about the case" (p. 16). Comparing the patient's account to an "unnavigable river," at one moment choked by rocks and at another divided and lost among sandbanks, he continues:

> They [the patients] can, indeed, give the physician plenty of coherent information about this or that period of their lives; but it is sure to be followed by another period as to which their communications run dry, leaving gaps unfilled, and riddles unanswered; and then again will come yet another period which will remain totally obscure and unilluminated by even a single piece of serviceable information. The connections—even the ostensible ones—are for the most part incoherent, and the sequence of different events is uncertain. Even during the course of their story patients will repeatedly correct a particular or a date, and then perhaps, after wavering for some time, return to their first version. The patients' inability to give an ordered history of their life in so far as it coincides with the history of their illness is not merely characteristic of the neurosis. It also possesses great theoretical significance. (pp. 16–17)

According to Freud, the inconsistencies, the gaps and lacunae, the ambiguities and the uncertainties of the neurotic patient's story are marks of repression. Neurotic patients are patients precisely because they are unable to represent themselves in the form of a consistent narrative. From this perspective, the aim of psychoanalytic therapy is to fill in the gaps in the patient's memory in order to (re)construct a coherent life story, or rather, in order to restore the patient's faculty of telling an ordered story of his own life. The psychoanalytic process is thus poised between two narratives: the patient's faulty story and another, more adequate, that is to say curative, story constituting the end of the therapeutic work: "It is only towards the end of the treatment that we have before us an intelligible, consistent, and unbroken case history" (p. 18).

Freud's introductory remarks are interesting, not only because he so explicitly describes the analytical process as a narrative process, or because he suggests that life, somehow, is structured as a consistent narrative, the difference between neurosis and mental health being the difference between the inconsistent and the ordered, coherent autobiographical account. They gain additional importance because there is an obvious discrepancy between, on the one hand, his ideal of an unbroken case story and, on the other hand, the inconsistency and the fragmentary nature of the case story he is about to report. Freud's analysis of Dora never reaches the point where the pieces of the puzzle fall into place; it never reaches the point where we are able to perceive a singular, intelligible pattern. Analyzing, in this case, seems to breed ambiguity; the more analysis, the less intelligibility. Rather than being the reconstruction of a story deformed by repression, Freud's reading of Dora is the production of "more story," no less obscure, enigmatic, and lacunary than the initial, neurotic narrative. *Fragment of an Analysis of a Case of Hysteria* never arrives at the promised dénouement.

After the completion, in 1901, of the greater part of the case story, Freud added a postscript in order to account for the fact that the case story remains (as he puts it) "incomplete to a far greater degree than its title might have led [the reader] to expect" (p. 112). In this postscript Freud introduces the concept of transference, which he, using a textual metaphor, defines as "new editions" of the fantasies revealed during the analytical process, or even (insofar as these fantasies have been subjected to a moderating influence) as "revised editions" (p. 116). Dora's unresolved transference—her identification of the analyst with Herr K.—caused her to break off the treatment prematurely. "I did not succeed in mastering the transference in good time," admits Freud (p. 118), as he looks back on the course of the analysis. In his commentary to the case, Jacques Lacan reverses this proposition by substituting countertransference for transference: "It is because he put himself rather too much in the place of Herr K. that . . . Freud did not succeed in moving the Acheron."[30] It is this dual theme of transference and countertransference subsequent commentators have pursued.

In the last part of the postscript, which reads as Freud's final effort to achieve some kind of closure, we are told that fifteen months after the case was over, "Dora came to see me again"; she came, writes Freud, "to finish her story" (p. 120). *Her* story? What characterizes this case is, it seems, precisely Freud's unwillingness to listen to this story. Her story is first of all articulated in the form of Dora's manifest resistance to the plot that Freud has conceived and her refusal to accept the role he has assigned to her. It is only between the lines of the story that Freud is determined to tell that we find traces of the one Dora has chosen for herself. Thus *Fragment of an Analysis of a Case of Hysteria* stages the unequal fight between two competing narrators, the analyst and his patient. As the case history advances, remarks Steven Marcus, "it becomes increasingly clear . . . that Freud and not Dora has become the central character in the action. . . . We begin to sense that it is his story that is being written and not hers that is being retold. Instead of letting Dora appropriate her own story, Freud became the appropriator of it.

The case history belongs progressively less to her than it does to him."[31]

Feminist critics dealing with this case have explored more thoroughly the relationship between this aggressive attempt, on the part of the analyst, to appropriate his patient's story and the cultural discourses, including concepts of femininity and of male and female sexuality, that prevented Freud from understanding Dora's hysteria. Stressing the connection between the kiss Herr K. presses on Dora (the kiss for which she, according to Freud, secretly craves) and the reconstruction the analyst tries to press on his patient, the feminist critics foreground the Lacanian notion of countertransference: "What did Freud want from Dora?"[32] In an important essay on the case, Toril Moi suggests that the fight for recognition between the two narrators, the male analyst and the female analysand, is in fact a power struggle between two epistemological models, between, on the one hand, Freud's (male) desire for closure and totality, his desire for the answers Dora supposedly withholds, and, on the other hand, Dora's model which—like the female body in psychoanalytic theory—"in Freud's vision emerge[s] as unfinished, diffuse, and fragmentary." Freud's discontent with the unfinished, broken case story betrays his dread of this fragmentary epistemological model. Suspended between the ideal of an "unbroken" story and the recognition of the incompleteness of the case, Freud's text, writes Moi, "oscillates endlessly between his desire for complete insight or knowledge and an unconscious realization (or fear) of the fragmentary, deferring status of knowledge itself."[33]

The notion of *Fragment of an Analysis of a Case of Hysteria* as a text that oscillates between different positions recurs in other critical discussions of this case. Marcus suggests that Freud's case story should be read as a literary work wavering between Victorianism and modernism.[34] According to Peter Brooks, who reads psychoanalysis in the light of narratology, the case of Dora occupies the position as a key text of transition in Freud's understanding of narrative. The discrepancy between the ideal of a consistent, intelligible, and unbroken case history and the failed analysis of Dora must be seen in the light of the discovery Freud was about to make, namely that the narrativizing at the heart of the psychoanalytic process is less simple than he believed it to be and "indeed inextricably bound up with the fictional."[35] *Fragment of an Analysis of a Case of Hysteria* marks Freud's dawning recognition of the fact that the adequate and curative narrative is not simply "there," waiting to be discovered and brought to light, but is the product of a process of telling and reading—a process that involves not just one but two narrators and two readers, the analyst and the analysand.

It was only after Freud had finished his treatment of Dora that he came to understand that the discursive recuperation of the past is played out in the constructed, artificial space of transference (and countertransference)—the space Brooks has characterized as a "un lieu fictif et semiotique"[36]—and that the analytical dialogue between analyst and analysand, rather than being the means for the recuperation of the story of the patient's past life, is inherently part of the content of this narrative. Thus the case of Dora points toward insights that find expression in subsequent case stories, notably in the case of the Wolf Man: the story of the patient's past life is a discursive and symbolic past, constructed in the course of the analytical process. The analytical narrative "exists only insofar as it is transmitted, insofar as it becomes part of a process of exchange,"[37] that is, insofar as it is transferred. The relation of the analytical narrative to the course of past events constituting the (absent) referent of the analytical narrative therefore remains anything but simple and unequivocal.

Brooks's discussion of the psychoanalytical process suggests that it is not enough to say that psychoanalysis is "implicitly a narratology."[38] One must add that Freud, in the course of his career, develops his understanding of narrativization in psychoanalysis, indeed, proceeds from one narrative theory to another that is far more complex and sophisticated. But must we necessarily assume the existence of an epistemological turning point in Freud's thinking? Must we necessarily distinguish between an "early" and a "late" Freud? The attempt to locate an epistemological break is certainly complicated by the repetitive structure of his thinking, that is, the fact that his later discoveries are prefigured in his writings from the nineties, and that he seems to abandon a hypothesis only to let it resurface in a slightly different form. Moreover, what characterizes Freud's work is precisely the complexity or the heterogeneity of his argument. A single text appears to authorize very different and even incompatible readings. It may, therefore, be more to the point to say that transition is a recurring event in Freud's thinking—that each text, in fact, implies an epistemological turning point. This, at least, is how I propose to read his essay "Constructions in Analysis," a text I shall refer to in the following as crucial to the understanding of strategies of reading in psychoanalysis and, indeed, to the understanding of psychoanalytic hermeneutics.

"Constructions in Analysis" appeared in 1937 and is thus one of Freud's last publications.[39] As the title indicates, the topic of this short paper is the analytical process. More precisely, it raises the question of the role of the analyst in this process. Much has been said about the role of the analysand and his work of free association. The discussion of the work of the analyst has, however, as Freud remarks, "been pushed into the background."[40] Focusing the attention on the task assigned to the analyst, "Constructions in Analysis" seeks to rectify the imbalance.

Yet the paper has an additional purpose: a "certain well-known man of science" has accused psychoanalysis of treating patients "upon the famous principle of 'Heads I win, tails you lose'"(p. 257); the analysand's rejection of a given interpretation is seen as an affirmation of its correctness, just as much as is his acceptance. "Constructions in Analysis" is an attempt to defend the psychoanalyst against this charge of imposing interpretations upon the patient. What is at stake is, in other words, the validity of psychoanalytic readings. Indeed, this essay revolves around the questions Spence raises in *Narrative Truth and Historical Truth:* What kind of truth-value does the analysis possess? What is the relationship between the patient's repressed history and the account produced in psychoanalytic therapy? What is the analyst in search of? As we shall see, no final answer is given to these questions. Freud seems to adopt two distinct or even opposing strategies in his attempt to defend the raison d'être of psychoanalysis. He seems to be moving from one concept of psychoanalytic truth to another and quite different one. Thereby, "Constructions in Analysis" becomes an original and quite remarkable contribution to the discussion of the psychoanalytic process and the general problem of reading in psychoanalysis.

As early as *Studies on Hysteria,* Freud described neurosis as a memory disease—the patients *"suffer mainly from reminiscences"*[41]—and has defined the aim of the analysis accordingly. The technique of psychoanalysis has changed over the years, Freud says in 1914, but the aim has "remained the same. Descriptively speaking, it is to fill in gaps in memory; dynamically speaking, it is to overcome resistances due to repression."[42] "Si la névrose est un temps perdu," Serge Viderman remarks, "la technique analytique a pour tâche de récupérer l'histoire."[43] This, in fact, is the stance Freud adopts on the first pages of "Constructions in Analysis." The analysand "must be brought to recollect certain experiences," he says. "What we are in search of is a picture of the patient's forgotten years that shall be alike trustworthy and in all essential respects complete" (pp. 257, 258). The point of departure of "Constructions in Analysis" is a definition of the object of psychoanalytic investigation that recalls Spence's conceptualizing of historical truth, but the argument brings the reader to a different conclusion.

Toward the end of the essay, Freud introduces *his* idea of historical truth, which turns out to be radically different from that of Spence. While historical truth, according to Spence, quite simply is "things as they really were," historical truth, in Freud's essay, can only be understood as what one might call a "reality effect." The line of argument in "Constructions in Analysis" takes the form of a series of almost imperceptible slidings or displacements. Emphasizing the patient's "forgotten years," Freud, on the opening pages, associates cure with the retrieval and reappropriation of the memory of certain traumatic experiences. Using Spence's terminology, we might paraphrase this proposition as "the bringing to light of the historical truth causes the symptom to disappear." By way of the introduction of the concept of construction in analysis, however, and through reflections on how to decide whether a construction is "correct" or "serviceable," Freud finally arrives at a concept of truth that may only hypothetically be deduced from an effect in the present. When the symptom disappears, it is implied, some kind of truth must have been obtained. But let me return to the beginning of "Constructions in Analysis" in order to retrace Freud's argument, step by step.

Traditional psychoanalytic therapy is often represented as a specific kind of one-way communication, a "talking cure" where the analysand does most of the talking. Maria Cardinal's autobiographical novel *Les mots pour le dire* is an example of this concept of psychoanalytic therapy.[44] The novel itself is a therapeutic process, represented as a monological work of recollection, a descent, layer by layer, into the repressed past, triggered by the analyst's refusal to listen to the patient/narrator's complaints about her physical symptoms. Throughout the book the analyst remains anonymous and almost completely silent. Indeed, his absence is an essential part of the treatment. The analyst provokes, precisely through his silence, a breakthrough of the unconscious voice in the patient's discourse; the stream of blood (the symptom) is replaced by a stream of (curative) words. The analysand talks, while the analyst listens—and gradually the former is brought to remember what she wanted to forget.

"Constructions in Analysis" begins by shaking this image of the psychoanalytic process. The patient should indeed be brought to remember that which he has repressed, but in this process the role of the analyst is not simply that of a catalyst. In fact, the repressed past is not brought to light by the patient through free association or through uncensored trains of memory; it is produced as a *construction* in analysis. Psychoanalytic therapy, Freud remarks, consists of two discrete voices and implies two active parties, the analysand and the analyst, to each of whom a distinct task is assigned. As is well known, the role of the analysand consists in relating memory fragments, thoughts, ideas, dreams, regardless of the seemingly unimportant nature of this material. The analyst, however, "has neither experienced nor repressed any of the material under consideration. . . . His task is to make out what has been forgotten from the traces which it has left behind or, more correctly, to *construct* it" (pp. 258–59; Freud's italics). While the business of the analysand is to produce the so-called raw material of the analysis, the task of the analyst is to utilize this material in his construction of the patient's forgotten past.

Freud makes a point of distinguishing between, on the one hand, "interpretation," or perhaps rather "deciphering" (*Deutung*), of an association or a dream element, for instance, and, on the other hand, "construction." To communicate a construction to a patient is to return to him a piece of his

> early history that he has forgotten, in some such way as this: "Up to your *n*th year you regarded yourself as the sole and unlimited possessor of your mother; then came another baby and brought you grave disillusionment. Your mother left you for some time, and even after her reappearance she was never again devoted to you exclusively. Your feelings towards your mother became ambivalent, your father gained a new importance for you," . . . and so on. (p. 261)

As this example clearly demonstrates, the construction is a narrative or a part of a narrative. A plot is outlined; events are arranged according to temporal sequence as well as to causal relationship: A paradisiacal, blissful mother-child symbiosis is interrupted by a crisis, the arrival of another baby. The protagonist partly loses his mother's attention and therefore turns to his father, and so on. To construct, then, is to fit the raw material of the analysis into a narrative scheme that implies a beginning, a middle, and an end. The construction is an attempt on the part of the analyst to place memory fragments in an order, and thus to establish the relationship between seemingly unrelated events. To construct is to plot.

Construction differs from *Deutung* insofar as the analytical construction is a hypothesis, based not only on the raw material produced by the analysand but also on psychoanalytic theory, the psychoanalytic metanarratives, as well as on the analyst's previous therapeutical experiences. To construct is to order and combine; but it is also an attempt to fill in gaps in memory. "I have restored what is missing," Freud says in his introduction to *Fragment of an Analysis of a Case of Hysteria*, "taking the best models known to me from other analyses; but, like a conscientious archaeologist, I have not omitted to mention in each case where the authentic parts end and my constructions begin" (p. 12). The analytical construction occupies an empty space, a silence, in the patient's discourse. It is a supplement to memory—and an indispensable supplement, indeed, because that which is missing is, as Freud points out, that which is most vital to the continuation of the analytical process. The scenes that are not reproduced during the treatment as recollections are precisely those that pertain to the patient's innermost secrets: scenes, dating from infancy, that are of essential importance to the case. The analytical construction, in other words, is necessitated by a blank or a void at the very center of the patient's being.

Needless to say, the theme of construction in analysis is a controversial issue. By conveying constructions to his patient, the analyst confronts the analysand with that which he does not—cannot—articulate, with that which he *fails* to remember. By filling in gaps in memory with a material that, in fact, does not belong to the analysand, the analyst enters his patient's discourse, takes over his voice, and assumes, as it were, the authority to speak on his behalf. Constructions thus foreground the artificial and precarious relationship that is established, in psychoanalytic therapy, between analyst and analysand: they belong within the "fictive" and "semiotic" space of transference and countertransference. Constructing is absolutely essential to the psychoanalytic process; without constructions we would never achieve anything, Freud has said. Yet, at the same time, the concept of construction in analysis raises a whole series of questions concerning the truth of psychoanalytic readings.

Having introduced the concept of construction in analysis, Freud hastens to assert the analyst's scientific right to construct. In *Fragment of an Analysis of a Case of Hysteria,* Freud, as we have seen, compares the analytical construction to the work of restoration carried out by the archaeologist; in "Constructions in Analysis" he adopts the same strategy. The analyst's "work of construction, or, if it is preferred, of reconstruction, resembles to a great extent an archaeologist's excavation of some dwelling-place that has been destroyed and buried or of some ancient edifice" (p. 259). Both of them, he continues, "have an undisputed right to reconstruct by means of supplementing and combining the surviving remains" (p. 259). Referring to constructions as restorations or reconstructions, he attempts to fit the concept of construction in analysis into the archaeological model of psychoanalysis. But the analogy between analytical construction and archaeological reconstruction is not allowed to stand. Toward the end of "Constructions in Analysis," Freud introduces another and far more surprising analogy: "I have not been able to resist the seduction of an analogy," he says. "The delusions of patients appear to me to be the equivalents of the constructions which we build up in the course of an analytic treatment—attempts at explanation and cure" (p. 268).

The archaeology model and the delusion model constitute different lines of argument in "Constructions in Analysis." Indeed, the juxtaposition of these two analogies raises the question whether analyt-ical constructions should be read as *re*constructions, in the sense of restorations, or as constructions, understood as productions of some-thing new. According to Spence, the difference between construction and reconstruction in the interpretative process parallels the differ-ence between narrative and historical truth.[45] But we do not have to subscribe to Spence's problematic concept of historical truth, as dis-tinct from narrative truth, in order to recognize in "Constructions in Analysis" different versions of the relationship between narrating and (his)story, or between the narrative constructed in analysis and the events of the past, and, consequently, to recognize different and even opposing concepts of analytical truth. According to the notion of con-struction as archaeological reconstruction, the task of the analyst is to uncover and restore an original and inherently meaningful series of recollections that faithfully represents the analysand's forgotten years. According to the analogy with the patient's delusions, construction is a creative and interpretive act pertaining to the past, but directed toward cure.

Indeed, the analogy with archaeology and the analogy with delu-sion present two different accounts of the relation of the psychoana-lytic process to time. From the perspective of the analogy between analytical construction and archaeological reconstruction, the past has priority. Meaning emerges from the past, or rather from the fragments of memory that have been uncovered in analysis and compel the analyst to draw certain conclusions as to the original arrangement of this material. The extent to which different pieces combine into a consistent whole becomes an indication of the correctness of the recon-struction. From the perspective of the analogy between construction and delusion, however, the emphasis is on the present of the analytical process and on the future cure. Meaning, or truth, seems to depend on the explanatory power of the construction and on its power to con-vince. According to the analogy with archaeology, the correct construc-tion is that which recaptures the past. The analogy between con-struction and delusion, however, suggests that the correct construction is that which produces a particular effect.

In order to understand Freud's analogy between construction and delusion, we should return to his opening discussion of the problem of verification in analysis. The analytical process is essentially dialogic. The analyst constructs a narrative or a piece of a narrative and conveys it to the analysand who, in turn, must accept or reject the construction he has been offered. The patient is, in other words, requested to verify the construction, but, as Freud remarks, this verification obviously cannot take the form of a simple "no" or a simple "yes"—"obviously," because the verification is in itself a paradox: the patient must accept or reject something of which he has no (conscious) memory. "It appears, therefore," Freud says, "that the direct utterances of the patient after he has been offered a construction afford very little evidence upon the question whether we have been right or wrong" (p. 263). Instead, the analyst must depend on "indirect forms of confirmation" (p. 263).

In "Constructions in Analysis" Freud distinguishes between two such types of indirect confirmation on the part of the patient. One is negative, an absence of reaction, so to speak: the patient remains completely untouched by the construction, and, Freud says, if nothing further develops in the course of the analysis, "we may conclude that we have made a mistake" (p. 261). The other type of reaction is positive, though not unambiguous: the patient himself becomes a constructor or narrator. He may answer by telling "something similar or analogous to the content of the construction" (p. 263). Or he may enter the narrative the analyst has constructed in order to complete and extend it; in other words, he becomes the conarrator of a story he cannot remember. In both cases, the construction is serviceable. The correct construction is that which proves capable of producing more story content. The successful analytical process is the interchange or interaction of two voices or two discourses. It is the production, in the fictive space of analysis, of a story that belongs, strictly speaking, neither to the analyst nor to the analysand, but to both. Two narrators tell the story of the patient's forgotten years, of the past to which neither analyst nor analysand has privileged access. The analytic construction, then, may be defined as a story created in the course of the analytical dialogue, a story that pertains to the patient's past, but which can only be symbolically verified in the present.

The analytical process is expected to lead up to the point where constructions are replaced by authentic memories of the patient's forgotten years. After all, constructions are fictions, surrogates; they ought to be replaced by the real thing. Freud never abandons his belief in the possibility of a total recovery of the past, that is, his belief (dating back to *Studies on Hysteria*) in the permanence of the past that has been preserved internally. Comparing the analytical process to the work of the archaeologist, Freud maintains that psychoanalysis, like archaeology, is the excavation of a past that has been preserved through burial. The only difference is that the analyst "works under more favorable conditions than the archaeologist" (p. 259). While the archaeologist must face the fact that parts of his object have been damaged or even destroyed, the object of psychoanalysis is indestructible. The past is still alive; it is still present in the form of memories that merely have become inaccessible to the subject. "Indeed, it may, as we know, be doubted whether any psychical structure can really be the victim of total destruction. It depends only upon analytic technique whether we shall succeed in bringing what is concealed completely to light" (p. 260).

While insisting on the indestructibility of the past and, consequently, on the possibility of a complete retrieval of the patient's forgotten years, Freud, in "Constructions in Analysis," nevertheless emphasizes that actual analyses every so often do not conform to this theory. "The path that starts from the analyst's construction ought to end in the patient's recollection; but it does not always lead so far. Quite often we do not succeed in bringing the patient to recollect what has been repressed" (p. 265). And he continues:

> Instead of that, if the analysis is carried out correctly, we produce in him an assured conviction of the truth of the construction which achieves the same therapeutic result as a recaptured memory. The problem of what the circumstances are in which this occurs and of how it is possible that what appears to be an incomplete substitute should nevertheless produce a complete result—all of this is matter for a later enquiry. (pp. 265–66)

In this quite remarkable passage Freud, at least momentarily, dissociates the issue of cause (the origin of the patient's neurosis) from the issue of (therapeutical) effect, that is, he dissociates the question of the authenticity of the account, created in the analytical dialogue, from the question of its ability to convince. The "psychoanalytic novel" has the power to produce a complete therapeutic result; cure, in fact, appears to depend less on the retrieval of authentic memories than on the patient's acceptance of the analytical construction. This new turn foregrounds the relationship established in the course of the analytical dialogue between analyst and analysand, since (as Freud remarks in *Fragment of an Analysis of a Case of Hysteria*) "it is only after the transference has been resolved that a patient arrives at a sense of conviction of the validity of the connections which have been constructed during the analysis" (p. 117). The treatment reaches a point where the narrative, created by two narrators in the analytical space of "as if," is taken over by the patient who, "after his resistances have been overcome, no longer invokes the absence of any memory of them [the constructed scenes], (any sense of familiarity with them) as a ground for refusing to accept them."[46]

The analytical construction is a supplement to or a substitute for memory, Freud points out. And yet it is not secondary; the therapeutic results that it produces are those of an authentic, recaptured memory.

The substitute assumes the same status and achieves the same effect as that which it is the substitute for. The narrative, constructed in analysis, works as if it were a recollection of the patient's forgotten years. It acts as if it were real; it assumes the effect of the real. The narrative of the past, constructed in the present of the analytical dialogue, is brought to fill the empty space in the analysand's memory; it becomes integrated with his own recollections, in the sense that it is accepted by the patient as the faithful account of his past, and works accordingly. The analytical construction becomes a "phantom memory," as it were. Indeed, at this point, we are concerned with a concept of truth very different from the one that provided the point of departure of "Constructions in Analysis": truth associated with the therapeutical effect, achieved as the construction comes to occupy an empty space in the patient's story and works as if it has always been there, rather than truth associated with the recuperation of original and authentic memories.

In the last few paragraphs of "Constructions in Analysis," Freud introduces his version of historical truth—a version, as I have already stated, that compels us to reconsider the Spencian notion of the term. First of all, in Spence's study, the term historical truth denotes a quite unproblematic concept of truth: "the 'way things were'" (p. 27). It should be emphasized that Freud, too, in his later works has coined an expression for this idea of an unproblematic, factual truth; he uses the term "material truth," which he, in *Moses and Monotheism*, distinguishes very sharply from the term "historical truth": "the *historical* truth and not the *material* truth."[47] In *Narrative Truth and Historical Truth,* Freud is criticized for confusing narrative truth with historical truth. But maybe it is Spence who confuses two kinds of truth, namely historical truth with material truth, by consistently associating the idea of a historical truth with Freud's belief that "in the process of psychoanalysis he was always uncovering *pieces* of the past."[48] Secondly, Spence's term "narrative truth" pertains to the phenomenon discussed above, namely, the observation that the narrative constructed in analysis acquires an explanatory power that allows it to function as if it were a recaptured memory or, in Spence's terminology, a "historical" reality. Paradoxically, it is precisely this observation that, in "Constructions in Analysis," causes Freud to advance his hypothesis of a historical truth. Freud's term may not be synonymous with Spence's term "narrative truth"; but perhaps the Freudian idea of historical truth is after all closer to Spence's idea of a narrative truth than Spence is prepared to admit.

As we have seen, Spence uses the term narrative truth to describe the phenomenon of an analytical construction that has become, qua its rhetorical appeal and its explanatory strength, just as real as any other kind of truth. "Narrative truth," he writes, "is what we have in mind when we say . . . that a given explanation carries conviction, that *one* solution to the mystery must be true" (p. 31). Freud, on his part, uses the term historical truth in connection with delusions and with semifictional constructions and ideas that possess an extraordinary persuasive strength. He uses the term in connection with those nonverifiable analytical constructions—substitutes—that produce a complete therapeutic result, as well as with ideas that acquire the effect of the real, even though they may be incompatible with actual, material reality. Historical truth pertains to that which "*must* be believed."[49] We may say that, in psychoanalysis, the notion of historical truth has the status of a referential hypothesis; the idea of "a fragment of historical truth" (p. 267) denotes an absent referent, knowable only through its effects. The assumption of a historical truth is Freud's attempt to account for an effect in the actual (cure, for instance) that he, in fact, cannot explain. Insofar as an analytical construction is capable of producing in the patient an assured conviction of its reality value—that is, insofar as it is capable of producing the same therapeutic effect as a recaptured memory—we must assume, Freud maintains, that this construction contains a fragment of historical truth: a fragment of truth, however, only knowable as an effect in the present, namely by the force of the conviction the construction conveys; a fragment of truth that may, indeed, be nothing *but* this effect in the present.

"Psychoanalytic concepts," writes Nicolas Abraham, "however awkward, or incoherent, or even outright scandalous they may appear, possess some sort of power, and one cannot include them in alien systems of reference without deadening their nerve."[50] This, surely, applies to Freud's complex notion of historical truth, which Spence has domesticated and simplified as he has lifted it out of its context in "Constructions in Analysis" and *Moses and Monotheism*. Rather than draw on the authority of history in order to convince us of the authenticity of psychoanalytic constructions, Freud has made strange and problematic what we believe we know under the name of historical truth.

From my discussion of "Constructions in Analysis" it has appeared that although I find Spence's definition of narrative truth, as opposed to historical truth, unsatisfactory or even misleading, I find it helpful to distinguish between different concepts of psychoanalytic interpretation in Freud's work, or rather between different ways of accounting for the psychoanalytic process and for reading in psychoanalysis in general. In the following two chapters I shall pursue this theme by outlining two different accounts of the psychoanalytic process: one that is conveyed by Freud's analogy between psychoanalysis and archaeology, and one that I will extract from Freud's famous case story of the Wolf Man, *From the History of an Infantile Neurosis*. It should be emphasized, however, that this structure, which suggests such a clear-cut distinction between different epistemological models, is purely provisional. For if Freud's work, as I will argue, contains different or even incompatible stories of reading, these stories co-exist, as "Constructions in Analysis" demonstrates, within the framework of even a single text.

Freud, in "Constructions in Analysis," arrives at a conception of the analytical process that problematizes his initial proposition that psychoanalysis shall bring to light "a picture of the patient's forgotten years" that is "in all essential respects complete." This conclusion, however, is not a result of a renunciation of his quest for origins and resignation to a Spencian concept of psychoanalytic interpretation as merely "a good story" (p. 31); rather, his argument reaches an impasse—that is, he runs up against a problem he can solve only by swerving from his initial line of thought. I have previously maintained that "Constructions in Analysis" contains an epistemological turning point. We may now locate this turning point in Freud's argument: it occurs as he, having discussed the patient's verification of the analytical construction, introduces one last problem—"Only one point requires investigation and explanation" (p. 265)—namely, the fact that an "incomplete substitute" may produce a "complete result" (p. 266). Now this is a recurrent moment in Freudian discourse: his line of argument leads to a final question that can only be answered at the risk of overthrowing previous conclusions. If psychoanalysis contains an alternative to Freud's story of psychoanalysis as an archaeology of the mind, this alternative story emerges from such daring and potentially disruptive moments in his thinking.

It has been argued that Freud's analogy with archaeology—which according to Spence pertains to his confusion of narrative truth with historical truth—belongs within "the wishful substratum" of his "scientific writings"; the analyst's self-image as archaeologist articulates the psychoanalytic dream of knowledge and explanatory power.[51] Toril Moi, in her discussion of the case of Dora, adopts a more explicitly critical stance on this point, as she highlights the connection between hermeneutical models and gender models in Freudian thinking. Figuring himself as an archaeologist, Freud claims that he has "restored what is missing" from Dora's fragmentary and lacunary story, which he compares to the "priceless though mutilated relics of antiquity."[52] But " 'the priceless though mutilated relics of antiquity' are not only Dora's story: they are Dora herself, her genitals and the feminine epistemological model. . . . Freud's task is therefore momentous: he must 're-store what is missing'; his penis must fill the epistemological hole represented by Dora." Freud's epistemology, argues Moi, is "clearly phallocentric."[53] It appears that the archaeological metaphor in psychoanalysis is inextricably bound up with Freud's (male) desire to fill up textual holes and gaps, his desire for narrative coherence and completeness, his desire for mastery.

The critique, on the part of literary critics and theorists, of Freud's "discourse of mastery," of his submission of the literary text to the authority of psychoanalysis, has been dealt with above. As a viable alternative to this (phallocentric) discourse of mastery, these critics propose a "discourse of mutual entanglement."[54] In the words of Shoshana Felman, the task of the psychoanalytic literary critic should be "to initiate a real exchange, to engage in a real *dialogue* between literature and psychoanalysis, as between two different bodies of language and between two different modes of knowledge."[55] As will become clear in the following, I subscribe to this critical enterprise. However, it should be recognized that the discourse of mastery is essential to psychoanalytic hermeneutics. As Susan Rubin Suleiman points out, unfortunately without pursuing the idea, "the desire 'to master the material'—whether it be dreams, the unconscious, the woman's body, sexual difference or narrative itself—was both *the generating impulse* and the Achilles' heel of the psychoanalytic project."[56] If Freud, as I have maintained, arrives at an account of interpretation in psychoanalysis that calls in question the analogy between psychoanalysis and archaeology, it is not because he has relinquished the dream of knowledge and interpretive authority that this figure articulates; on the contrary, his deconstruction of the archaeological metaphor is an effect of the desire for explanatory mastery. It is precisely Freud's quest for knowledge and his belief that everything may be analyzed and explained that, again and again, will cause him to press his argument to the point where it turns against itself. To cut away the desire for mastery is, I think, to cut away the critical potentials of psychoanalytic hermeneutics.

It has been stated that traditional psychoanalytic criticism, by its very nature, is authoritarian or even imperialistic.[57] But is this in fact the case? It seems to me that these psychoanalytic critics have not been sufficiently imperialistic; contrary to Freud, they have not ventured to attempt an extension of the limits of the analyzable, but contented themselves with posing the questions to which they believed they had the answers. This, I think, is the reason why Freud's literary interpretations, "bad" as they may be, invariably seem more interesting to us than the kind of readings often evoked by the term "psychoanalytic literary criticism." Freud's readings of fictional texts continue to engage readers, not because these readings claim absolute hermeneutical authority or because they pretend to be the answer to the textual question, but because, as the ultimate consequence of Freud's quest for the final answer, there is always one more—unsettling and potentially disruptive—question, always one more point that requires investigation and explanation. The critical force of Freud's readings depends on the fact that his will to interpretive power invariably compels him to go beyond the merely satisfactory reading.

Part Two
Stories of Reading

Chapter 2

Gradiva: **Psychoanalysis as Archaeology**

In 1907 Freud published *Delusions and Dreams in Jensen's* Gradiva, an interpretation in light of psychoanalysis of a short novel by the German writer Wilhelm Jensen, *Gradiva: Ein Pompejanisches Phantasiestück,* which had appeared in 1903.[1] *Delusions and Dreams in Jensen's* Gradiva is Freud's most extensive reading of a literary text, and yet this essay has largely been overlooked by literary critics.[2] This choice may seem well justified: from the perspective of literary criticism, the crudely naive, "realistic" approach Freud adopts is obviously unsatisfactory. Besides, as Freud himself admits, *Gradiva* is not a particularly valuable work of literature. However, one should not forget that the primary objective of the essay is neither to outline a psychoanalytic approach to literature nor to establish a psychoanalytic theory of art. In *Delusions and Dreams in Jensen's* Gradiva Freud suggests a relationship between literature on the one hand and psychoanalysis on the other, yet it is psychoanalysis rather than literature that is the topic of his discussion. Freud construes Jensen's narrative as a psychoanalytic novel—and he does so with the explicit intention of pronouncing *Gradiva* the ally of psychoanalysis. Within the context of Freud's work, *Gradiva* is called upon to confirm the truth of psychoanalytic interpretation. But which truth? The present chapter is an attempt to answer this question.

It was Carl Jung who first called attention to Jensen's story of the young archaeologist, Norbert Hanold, who falls in love with an ancient relief representing a woman with a particularly graceful gait. Three dreams are embedded in this colorful narrative. Would it be possible, asked Jung, to interpret these fictive dreams, "dreams that have never been dreamt at all," in the same way as actual dreams?[3] In *Delusions and Dreams in Jensen's* Gradiva, Freud accepts Jung's challenge and undertakes a psychoanalytic interpretation of the dreams "dreamt" by the main character of Jensen's novel. The implied reader of Freud's essay, however, is not so much his friend and disciple as those scientists who have previously rejected the notion of the dream as a meaningful mental phenomenon to be interpreted scientifically or systematically. Freud turns *Gradiva* into an argument in support of *The Interpretation of Dreams*. "Science and the majority of educated people smile if they are set the task of interpreting a dream," Freud says with a touch of bitterness (p. 7). But psychoanalysis, he continues, has at least one "ally": the poet who knows "a whole host of things between heaven and earth of which our philosophy has not yet let us dream" (p. 8). The poet appears "to be on the same side as . . . the author of *The Interpretation of Dreams*" (p. 8); the poet, too, considers dreams to be meaningful and related to our waking life.

What is at stake is thus the question of the readability of dreams. Freud turns to the literary text, *Gradiva,* in order to prove that he is right. *Delusions and Dreams in Jensen's* Gradiva may be read as one long defense of the dream theory, or rather a defense of psychoanalysis as such, because, as it turns out, he is unable to separate his interpretation of the three dreams in *Gradiva* from his analysis of the delusion to which the protagonist falls victim. Norbert Hanold, on a visit to Pompeii, encounters a young woman who bears a striking resemblance to Gradiva, the name that he has chosen for the relief. The archaeologist believes this woman to be a ghost—the model of his work of art who has returned from the land of the dead—and he is only set free from this delusion when the young woman reveals herself to be Zoe, his childhood sweetheart and neighbor in Germany whose existence he had apparently forgotten. The dreams, it is maintained, are only comprehensible within this context of "the formation and the cure of the delusions" (p. 92), of which Jensen, says Freud, has given a correct description. The author, in other words, does not merely agree with the psychoanalyst on the issue of the readability of dreams. Although he confesses not to have read the work of Freud,[4] Jensen has given a faithful (albeit poetical) representation of the formation of dreams and symptoms, that is, of the laws of the unconscious, as well as a correct impression of the methodological principles of psychoanalytic therapy.

Indeed, the author of *Gradiva* possesses a profound psychoanalytic knowledge. Having transcribed *Gradiva* into a psychoanalytic novel, Freud concludes that "I myself have supported all the views that I have here extracted from Jensen's *Gradiva* and stated in technical terms" (p. 53). "[T]he author has expressly renounced the portrayal of reality by calling his story a 'phantasy.' We have found, however, that all his descriptions are so faithfully copied from reality that we should not object if *Gradiva* were described not as a phantasy but as a psychiatric study" (p. 41). Freud may therefore conclude his interpretation by establishing that "either both of us, the writer and the doctor, have misunderstood the unconscious in the same way, or we have both understood it correctly. This conclusion is of great value to us" (p. 92).

Independently of each other, the poet and the psychoanalyst have discovered the laws of the unconscious. The content of *Gradiva* is thus claimed to be psychoanalysis, or rather, as I argue, a particular interpretation of psychoanalysis. For what exactly do Freud and Jensen agree upon? The answer is to be sought in the relationship, suggested by the novel, between on the one hand the formation and the cure of Norbert Hanold's delusion, and the fate of Pompeii, its burial and subsequent excavation, on the other. The archaeologist in a dream sees Gradiva in Pompeii, on the very day of the fatal eruption of Vesuvius that buried the town and its inhabitants under masses of lava. This dream marks the onset of his delusion from which he is cured as he recovers his long-forgotten love among the excavated ruins of Pompeii. Without having read Freud's work, Jensen based his narrative upon an analogy Freud himself had made use of since the 1890s: the analogy between the archaeological excavation and the retrieval of a seemingly forgotten past. The alliance between the psychoanalyst and the author of the "Pompeian Fantasy" is contained within the more comprehensive alliance, suggested by Freud, between psychoanalysis and archaeology. Freud is able to read *Gradiva* as proof of the insights of psychoanalysis, because he himself has already referred to archaeology in order to support the claims of psychoanalysis to truthfulness, or rather, because his idea of psychoanalytic truth is always already marked by archaeology as epistemological paradigm. What Freud and Jensen agree upon is the concept of psychoanalysis as an archaeology of the soul.

Freud coined the archaeological metaphor in the nineties—the decade that saw the appearance of a psychoanalytic therapeutic method, developed from Breuer's cathartic method, as well as the formulation of basic psychoanalytic theories—and versions of this figure continued to haunt his writings. Explicit references to archaeology and archaeological discoveries appear in many of his works, including *Studies on Hysteria* (1893–95), "The Aetiology of Hysteria" (1896), *Fragment of an Analysis of a Case of Hysteria* (1905), *Notes upon a Case of Obsessional Neurosis* (1909), *Civilization and Its Discontents* (1930), "Constructions in Analysis" (1937), and *Moses and Monotheism* (1939). Hidden or implicit references, however, are everywhere. Archaeology is part of the language of psychoanalysis, or perhaps of the metalanguage of psychoanalysis, the language in which psychoanalysis represents itself as a depth psychology or a depth hermeneutics—an uncovering, a bringing to light, an unearthing, or an excavation of a hidden reality.

Far from being a purely ornamental or didactic feature, a simile called upon to illustrate, but in itself outside psychoanalytic discourse proper and separable from psychoanalytic thinking as such, the analogy with archaeology is inextricably bound up with the attempt to explain the objectives and methods of psychoanalytic interpretation, that is, with the attempt to provide a systematic, coherent account of the psychoanalytic process. Freud himself recognized that his metaphors were more than mere ornaments. He was aware of the fact that "in psychology we can only describe things by the help of analogies."[5] "We could not otherwise describe the processes in question at all, and indeed we could not have become aware of them."[6] As is well known, the language of psychoanalysis is densely figurative. Yet, among the rich variety of analogies and metaphors in Freud's writings, none has provided a stronger, more comprehensive, and more seductive account of reading in psychoanalysis, and none has proved more persistent than the archaeological metaphor that firmly anchors psychoanalysis in nineteenth-century epistemology.[7]

Paul Ricoeur's comprehensive outline of psychoanalytic hermeneutics has stressed the importance of the archaeological metaphor in Freudian thinking. "Freudianism is an explicit and thematized archaeology," he writes; "psychoanalysis is an archaeology; it is an archaeology *of the subject*."[8] But what does it mean to conceive of psychoanalysis in terms of an archaeology of the soul? To open the discussion we may turn to the writings of the nineties. In 1896 Freud delivered a lecture before the *Verein für Psychiatrie und Neurologie,* in which he argued that the new method of psychoanalysis has succeeded in shifting attention from the hysterical symptoms to a knowledge of their hidden causes. The hysterical symptom, he pointed out, arises in connection with an event that seems to lack both suitability to serve as a determinant and traumatic force. Behind this event, however, the memory of another scene is concealed, the memory of an early "pre-sexual sexual" traumatic experience, the true cause or origin of the hysterical attack.

In a letter to his friend Wilhelm Fliess, Freud described the *Verein*'s reaction to this theory as being "icy." "In defiance of my colleagues," he continued in a second letter, "I have written out my lecture on the aetiology of hysteria" for publication.[9] Here is how Freud, on the opening pages of this essay, "The Aetiology of Hysteria," introduces the psychoanalytic method:

> But in order to explain . . . the method which we have to employ . . . I should like to bring before you an analogy taken from

an advance that has in fact been made in another field of work. Imagine that an explorer arrives in a little-known region where his interest is aroused by an expanse of ruins, with remains of walls, fragments of columns, and tablets with half-effaced and unreadable inscriptions. He may content himself with inspecting what lies exposed to view, with questioning the inhabitants—perhaps semibarbaric people—who live in the vicinity, about what tradition tells them of the history and meaning of these archaeological remains, and with noting down what they tell him—and he may then proceed on his journey. But he may act differently. He may have brought picks, shovels and spades with him, and he may set the inhabitants to work with these implements. Together with them he may start upon the ruins, clear away the rubbish, and, beginning from the visible remains, uncover what is buried. If his work is crowned with success, the discoveries are self-explanatory: The ruined walls are part of the ramparts of a palace or a treasure-house; the fragments of columns can be filled out into a temple; the numerous inscriptions, which, by good luck, may be bilingual, reveal an alphabet and a language, and, when they have been deciphered and translated, yield undreamed-of information about the events of the remote past, to commemorate which the monuments were built. *Saxa loquuntur!*[10]

The nineteenth century was obsessed with the relationship—the disjunction—between "surfaces" and "depths," between appearances and that which is beneath or inside. Applying the archaeological narrative to the description of the work of analysis, Freud situates his own enterprise within this epistemological surface/depth paradigm. The distinguishing mark of the psychoanalytic method is precisely that it does not content itself with remaining on the surface, but penetrates to that which is hidden underneath, the remote past conceived as depth. In dealing only with that which lies exposed to view, one finds nothing but incoherent and unreadable fragments—fragments, however, that ultimately, as one descends into deeper layers of the past, will prove to be meaningful signs that combine into intelligible words and sentences. The movement from surface to depth, from present to past, is thus a movement from part to whole, from apparent inconsistency, incoherence, and unreadability to coherence and plenitude of meaning. *Saxa loquuntur*—stones talk!

Comparing the hysterical patient's symptoms to scattered and incomprehensible remains of an ancient culture, Freud pictures himself as an archaeologist who gradually works his way through layers of time. The archaeologist and the psychoanalyst are twin explorers in an unknown region. Both proceed by way of excavation, deciphering, and reconstruction. Both throw light on the archaic, be it the prehistory of human civilization or the infantile origins of neurosis. It follows that the analogy with archaeology is not only an attempt to provide an account of the psychoanalytic process, but is, by the same token, a statement about the authenticity of that which is revealed in the course of this process. I am not merely referring to the reality or the truth of infantile seduction scenes; significantly, the analogy with archaeology and the claims to truth and scientific objectivity implicit in this analogy outlive the seduction theory (which Freud privately renounced as early as 1897). What is at stake is the authority of psychoanalysis itself, the validity of psychoanalytic interpretation. Essential to the self-image of the psychoanalyst is the assumption that analysis, as Ricoeur puts it, at the end of its process of deciphering, "reaches a reality just as much as do stratigraphy and archaeology."[11]

It is hardly surprising that the analogy with archaeology suggested itself to the founder of psychoanalysis. As is well known, Freud himself was a passionate collector of antique artifacts. A passage from *Notes upon a Case of Obsessional Neurosis* shows how he brought his collection of antiquities to bear on the analytical process. In this case story Freud relates how he, in explaining the principles of psychoanalysis to his patient, made "some short observations upon *the psychological differences between the conscious and the unconscious.*" "I illustrated my remarks," he continues, "by pointing to the antiques standing about in my room."[12] The archaeological metaphor was thus staged or materialized, so to speak, in the very rooms that provided the setting of the analytical dialogue—those rooms which, as Suzanne Bernfeld observes, "finally took on the look of a museum."[13] The analytical "excavation" was carried out in sight of Egyptian, Roman, and Greek grave finds, and the analyst's finds were symbolically added to the collection of ancient objects that in turn provided a visible material counterpart to those uncovered by the analyst.

Freud's interest in archaeology exceeded that of the art collector. "I . . . have actually read more archaeology than psychology," he jokingly remarked in a letter to Stefan Zweig,[14] and as the Fliess correspondence demonstrates, this interest dates back to the formative years of psychoanalysis. Carl Schorske, in *Fin-de-Siècle Vienna,* describes these years as follows:

> Like most cultivated Austrians of his generation Freud was steeped
> in classical culture. Once he hit upon the analogy between his work
> as depth psychologist and the work of an archaeologist, his mild

interest flowered into a burning passion for antiquity. He consumed with avidity Jacob Burckhardt's newly published *History of Greek Culture*, so rich in materials on primitive myth and religion. He read with envy the biography of Heinrich Schliemann who fulfilled a childhood wish by his discovery of Troy. Freud began the famous collection of ancient artifacts which were to grace his office in the Berggasse. And he cultivated a new friendship in the Viennese professional elite—especially rare in those days of withdrawal—with Emanuel Löwy, a professor of archaeology. "He keeps me up till three o'clock in the morning," Freud wrote appreciatively to Fliess, "He tells me about Rome."[15]

The nineteenth century, and especially the last decades, saw a number of striking archaeological discoveries, of which the most sensational no doubt were Schliemann's excavation of Troy, as well as his work at Mycenae and Tiryns, and the uncovering and reconstruction of Knossos directed by the British archaeologist John Evans. Like so many of his contemporaries Freud participated in these excavations "by following in the newspapers and journals their progress in Pompeii, Rome and Troy."[16] But to the founder of psychoanalysis, the major archaeological discoveries of the late nineteenth century had a special meaning. As Schorske points out, Freud admired and envied Heinrich Schliemann, the German amateur archaeologist who, much to the amazement of the archaeological establishment, succeeded in bringing to light an ancient city he declared to be the Homeric Troy. And it is hardly a coincidence that Freud's analogy with archaeology in "The Aetiology of Hysteria"—a paper written out "in defiance of my colleagues"—reads as a condensed version of precisely Schliemann's account of how he excavated Troy and thus silenced the experts who had repudiated his theory of the site of Homer's city.[17]

The great archaeological discoveries of the late nineteenth century affirmed the idea of the possibility of retrieving a seemingly lost past. Thus Schliemann, as well as Evans, succeeded in bringing to light surprisingly well-preserved remains of a forgotten culture. And, as they recognized the importance of reporting their discoveries to the general public, both archaeologists wrote extensive narrative accounts of the progress of their excavations. "Have you read that the English have excavated an old palace in Crete (Knossos) which they declare to be the original labyrinth of Minos?" wrote Freud in a letter to Fliess (1901).[18] The following description of the bringing to light of the fresco of the Cupbearer is excerpted from Evans's own account of these excavations:

The colours were almost as brilliant as when laid down over three thousand years ago. For the first time the true portraiture of a man of this mysterious Mycenaean race rises before us. There was something very impressive in this vision of brilliant youth and of male beauty, recalled after so long an interval to our upper air from what had been till yesterday a forgotten world.[19]

The Fliess correspondence shows that Freud's concept of the psychoanalytic process from the very beginning was bound up with the rhetoric of such archaeological narratives. As the archaeologists themselves saw it, the excavation of Troy and Knossos brought myth into the realm of reality. The work of Schliemann and Evans suggested to the archaeologists that "there is doubtless a kernel of historical truth in most of the old Greek legends,"[20] and Freud saw his own psychoanalytic project reflected in this discovery. If a kernel of historical truth can be found in the ancient legends and myths of a given culture, why should not this apply to the myths and legends of an individual, that is, to the fantasies and dreams that form the psychoanalyst's object of study? And since the archaeologists, in Schliemann's words, had succeeded "in penetrating to the deepest darkness of pre-historic times,"[21] why should it not be possible for psychoanalysis to uncover the prehistory of the subject? Reporting to Fliess the advances of his latest analysis, Freud wrote: "Buried deep beneath all his [the patient's] phantasies we found a scene from his primal period (before twenty-two months) which meets all requirements and into which all the surviving puzzles flow." The letter, which is dated December 12, 1899, continues as follows: "It is everything at the same time—sexual, innocent, natural, etc. I can hardly bring myself to believe it yet. It is as if Schliemann had dug up another Troy which had hitherto been believed to be mythical."[22]

In the light of Freud's comparison of the scenes of infancy with Schliemann's Troy, psychoanalysis would appear to be not a new and suspect enterprise but rather the attempt to expand the archaeological project to the field of the individual psyche. Indeed, this, I think, was how Freud, around the turn of the century, perceived his own work. One may of course argue that it was the tangible reality of the archaeological find that made the analogy with archaeology so alluring to the psychoanalyst: by comparing the scenes from infancy that were brought to light in the analytical process to the excavated remains of Troy, Freud lent substance to his findings, so to speak. But, certainly, this is not the entire story. The archaeological metaphor has several dimensions, and Freud probably perceived not just a similarity but

also a more immediate relationship between archaeology and psychoanalysis.

In the course of the nineteenth century the (remote) past assumed
a new significance as key to the understanding of the present. In this
period, Peter Brooks argues,

> not only history but historiography, the philosophy of history,
> philology, mythography, diachronic linguistics, anthropology, ar-
> chaeology, and evolutionary biology all establish their claim as
> fields of inquiry, and all respond to the need for an explanatory
> narrative that seeks its authority in a return to origins and the
> tracing of a coherent story forward from origin to present.[23]

In this respect, the excavation of the "layered" Troy was not merely a
sensational archaeological drama; this discovery in significant ways
contributed to the dating of archaeological findings in the entire Medi-
terranean area. And, indeed, the problem of determining the relative
age of a find was the problem that most occupied the nineteenth-
century archaeologist. The appearance of methods for dating, classify-
ing, and contextualizing the archaeological find responded as well as
contributed to the predominant historical orientation of the century.
The archaeological object itself acquired a new meaning; it became a
readable sign, a clue to the origin and development of human civilization. Typological methods—the study of the evolution of form, inspired by evolutionary biology—as well as methods of dating derived
from geology and stratigraphy, allowed the archaeologist to perceive
the objects unearthed not as detached artifacts but as parts of a comprehensible whole, as traces of a process that may be mapped. From
having been a mere treasure hunt, archaeology, in the course of the
nineteenth century, became a field of study that could define its objective as follows: "To ascertain the original form both of the general plan
and its separate part, to follow the successive alterations that have come
in the course of time, to assign to each detail its place in the development, and thus to make the excavation a reconstruction of the lost
whole."[24]

No doubt Freud saw psychoanalysis as the extension of the epistemological project of archaeology, geology, evolutionary biology, and
other sciences to the study of the psyche. In this respect psychoanalysis
is a manifestation of that which Brooks describes as "the nineteenth
century's obsession with questions of origin, evolution, progress, genealogy."[25] In psychoanalysis the return to the past is motivated and
justified by the assumption that present behavior is fully comprehensi-

ble only in the light of the past. The infantile past is assumed to contain within it causes for the present, be it the present of the patient's symptoms or the present of adult sexuality. The archaeological model suggests that detection of scenes from the primeval period will enable the psychoanalyst to retrace human psychosexual development and, in so doing, to throw new light on the present. From this perspective Freud's reference to archaeology may be seen as an attempt to apply the objectives of the new archaeological science, as stated above, to the study of the individual mind or of the mental apparatus in general, that is, as an attempt to provide, by means of the excavation of fragments of individual prehistory, a systematic account of psychic development.

It follows that the history of archaeology in the nineteenth and the beginning of the twentieth century is more than just the account of a series of fabulous archaeological excavations but also the history of the birth of a new discipline. At the beginning of the nineteenth century, archaeology was little more than an unsystematic collecting of antiquities; by the turn of the century it had established itself as a scientific field of inquiry. The nineteenth century saw the appearance of an entirely new field of study, namely prehistory,[26] as well as the development of more systematic methods of excavation and new techniques in conservation and preservation. Consequently, a new type of archaeologist emerged. In fact, Schliemann may be seen as the last representative of the successful amateur archaeologist:

> In the course of the nineteenth century, archaeology became a science. It acquired full awareness of its own nature and objectives, with the establishment of the experimental method also applied to historical studies. . . . Exploration and excavation could no longer be left, as hitherto, to the discretion of amateurs, rich patrons, or adventurers. These activities had to be disciplined in a program of systematic work carried out in accordance with precise scientific directives.[27]

Freud's admiration for Schliemann and his Homeric adventure is proverbial. Yet he also drew upon the progress in archaeological techniques in order to illustrate the advances in the field of psychoanalysis. And on the whole it makes sense, I think, to see the growth of archaeology into a discipline, which by the turn of the century thought of itself as a science, as an emblem of Freud's idea of the development of psychoanalytic methods of investigation. In the later years of his career, Freud preferred to identify with the archaeologist-as-scientist, preoccupied with the problem of reconstructing and dating the archaeological find, rather than with the image of the archaeologist as "explorer in a little-known region." Take, for instance, the following passage from "Constructions in Analysis" (1937):

> One of the most ticklish problems that confronts the archaeologist is notoriously the determination of the relative age of his finds; and if an object makes its appearance in some particular level, it often remains to be decided whether it belongs to that level or whether it was carried down to that level owing to some subsequent disturbance. It is easy to imagine the corresponding doubts that arise in the case of analytic constructions. (p. 259)

What we have here is a more sophisticated notion of the work of the archaeologist; the discoveries are no longer assumed to be "self-explanatory" (as Freud put it in 1896). However, the role of the archaeological metaphor within psychoanalytic discourse has essentially remained the same. Through the reference to archaeology Freud affirms the possibility of rediscovering the past, just as he affirms that the reality that forms the object of psychoanalytic investigation exists prior to and independently of the work of analysis itself.

Mythography, philology, anthropology, evolutionary biology, and archaeology: each of these related fields of inquiry contributed to Freud's thinking; each of these disciplines contributed to the figurative language of psychoanalysis. Yet archaeology was—and is—particularly suggestive, first of all because this metaphor provided psychoanalysis with an alluring spatial model of the unconscious.

> [I]t came about that in this, the first full-length analysis of a hysteria [Fräulein Elizabeth von R., 1892] undertaken by me, I arrived at a procedure which I later developed into a regular method and employed deliberately. This procedure was one of clearing away the pathogenic psychical material layer by layer, and we liked to compare it with the technique of excavating a buried city. I would begin by getting the patient to tell me what was known to her and I would carefully note the points at which some train of thought remained obscure or some link in the causal chain seemed to be missing. And afterwards I would penetrate into deeper layers of her memories at these points by carrying out an investigation under hypnosis or by the use of some similar technique. The whole work was, of course, based on the expectation that it would be possible to establish a completely adequate set of determinants for the events concerned.[28]

Picturing the organization of memories as a stratified or layered structure (similar to the layered structure of Troy, for instance), Freud, in this passage from *Studies on Hysteria,* equates age with depth. The deepest strata contain also the most ancient material. The "fact that the scenes are uncovered in a reversed chronological order . . . justifies our comparison of the work with the excavation of a stratified ruined site."[29] (It is no contradiction of this model that he later, in "Constructions in Analysis," will take into account the possibility that the material in question may have been "carried down to that level owing to some subsequent disturbance.") Analysis, accordingly, is the act of peeling away layers of time; it is a descent into the depths of the patient's past, which has been preserved internally.

The analogy with archaeology reads time as (stratified) space; it provides Freud with a spatiotemporal model that is, by the same token, a model of "preservation in the sphere of the mind."[30] The repressed past is contained and preserved within; it is an unchanging or a timeless content, only in need of discovery to be brought to light. A passage (also excerpted above) from *Notes upon a Case of Obsessional Neurosis* reads:

> I then made some short observations upon *the psychological differences between the conscious and the unconscious,* and upon the fact that everything conscious was subject to a process of wearing-away, while what was unconscious was relatively unchangeable; and I illustrated my remarks by pointing to the antiques standing about in my room. They were, in fact, I said, only objects found in a tomb, and their burial had been their preservation: the destruction of Pompeii was only beginning now that it had been dug up. . . . The unconscious, I explained, *was* the infantile; it was that part of the self which had become separated off from it in infancy, which had not shared the later stages of its development, and which had in consequence become *repressed.* (pp. 176–77; Freud's italics)

The analogy with archaeology here suggests the existence of two different kinds of psychic temporality, defined through the distinction between surface and depth, between that which lies exposed and that which is hidden, concealed, or buried. On the one hand we have the temporality of consciousness, on the other hand the atemporality of the unconscious. Conscious material is transitory; it is submitted to the process of decay and destruction. Through the process of repression, such material may be separated off and buried. But burial at the same time means preservation and survival; by virtue of repression psychic material escapes the fate of "wearing away" to which everything conscious is subject.

The antiques have been preserved for posterity, precisely because they have been buried; the infantile past, likewise, remains intact because it has been encrypted in the unconscious in a state of repression. "There is, in fact," Freud says, "no better analogy for repression, by which something in the mind is at once made inaccessible and preserved, than burial of the sort to which Pompeii fell a victim and from which it could emerge once more through the work of spades."[31] In psychoanalysis, he writes elsewhere,

> we are regularly met by a situation which with the archaeological object occurs only in such rare circumstances as those of Pompeii or of the tomb of Tut'ankhamun. All of the essentials are preserved; even things that seem completely forgotten are present somehow and somewhere, and have merely been buried and made inaccessible to the subject.[32]

Accordingly, forgetting, strictly speaking, applies only to the conscious (and preconscious) system. Repression, it is maintained, is a most perfect albeit a most peculiar form of memory. Nothing is lost, yet nothing is present. The archaeological model of burial-as-preservation allowed the analyst to conceive of psychic material as being at the same time absent and present, forgotten and permanently inscribed in memory.

The archaeological metaphor implies the idea of the past as preserved internally, that is, the idea of the persistence of the subjective past as well as of the possibility of its coming to light. We may read this figure as the return of a Romantic image—as the return of the Romantic notion that "Everlasting layers of ideas, images, feelings, have fallen upon our brain softly as light. Each succession has seemed to bury all that went before. And yet, in reality, not one has been extinguished."[33] By reading time as inner space, by representing the personal past as mental depth, the Romantics defended themselves against the anxiety of loss or fragmentation of the self, of oblivion and death, and of temporality itself. Making the most remote past coefficient to our most intimate depth is a way of refusing loss and separation, claims Jean Starobinski in his study of the Romantic idea of lived time, "*le vécu*," as mental depth stratum; it is a way of "preserving, in the crammed plenum we imagine history to be, every moment spent along the way." And he continues,

> To say that the individual constructed himself through his history is to say that the latter is cumulatively present in him and that even

as it was elapsing, it was becoming internal structure. From this idea one cannot but draw an inference and its corollary, the inference being that self-knowledge is anamnesis or rememoration, and the corollary that anamnesis is the recognition of deep layers (often compared to geological strata) of the present-day person.[34]

As the works of Wordsworth, Coleridge, and de Quincey demonstrate, the Romantic poets showed a marked concern with the workings of memory, including extreme forms of memory such as, for instance, paramnesia, which is the topic of Georges Poulet's essay from 1954 with the suggestive title "Timelessness and Romanticism." Paramnesia seems to bring forth a past that is still real; paramnesia seems to project the subject into "a timeless world or into a world where time does not flow but stands still." The implication of paramnesia is the "incredible idea that all the past we thought we had left for ever, continues to stay here, at our very feet, invisible but intact, and in all its forgotten freshness, shoots forth into our minds." We come here, Poulet contends,

> to the essential belief of Coleridge, and moreover of nearly all the Romanticists, the belief in the continued existence of the past, in the wonderful possibilities of its revival. Nothing is lost. All our life, and especially all our childhood, with all our perceptions, images and feelings, and whatever ideas we have had, persists in our mind.[35]

But if Freud's analogy with archaeology was the return of a Romantic figure, it was the return of this figure as other. The Romantic idea that nothing is lost, the idea of a hidden timeless world, made its return in Freudian discourse in the form of the theory of the persistence or permanence of that which one most wanted to forget. And what may be more important in this context: to Freud, the idea of the buried past carried the full weight of the technical sophistication that archaeology, in the course of the nineteenth century, had achieved; it implied the idea of the possibility of a systematic excavation of the past. The passage from Poulet quoted above continues: "but as we are living in duration, it is not permitted to us to have anything but rare glimpses, disconnected reminiscences, of this immense treasure stored in a remote place in our soul" (p. 11). In contrast, the image of "the buried city" to Freud entailed the image of "the work of spades," the idea of psychoanalysis as "a procedure," "a regular method," or a "technique of excavating a buried city."[36] As he contends in "Constructions in

Analysis": "It depends only upon analytic technique whether we shall succeed in bringing what is concealed completely to light" (p. 260). In psychoanalysis, the analogy with archaeology is first and foremost a statement on the possibility of retrieving through systematic analysis a seemingly forgotten past.[37]

As a story of burial, preservation, and subsequent excavation, the analogy with archaeology offers a persuasive account of the psychoanalytic process as related to the process of repression—an account of dissociation and reintegration, or of a presence that is turned into an absent presence yet ultimately becomes present once again. In his study of the psychoanalytic dialogue, Roy Schafer suggests that psychoanalysis may be read as a set of narratives (or perhaps rather metanarratives) that determine the course of the analytical process and the ways of representing this process. "Far from being secondary narratives about data, these structures provide primary narratives that establish what is to count as data," claims Schafer; the data of psychoanalysis should unfailingly be "regarded as constituted rather than simply encountered."[38]

It might be useful to think of the analogy with archaeology as just such a narrative of the analytical process and of the psychoanalytic reading of the past. However, the message this narrative conveys is precisely that the material produced in the psychoanalytic process is "encountered" rather than "constituted." Representing the psychoanalytic process as a symmetrical reversal, as it were, of the process of repression (repression as burial, analysis as excavation), the analogy between the work of the archaeologist and the work of the psychoanalyst tells a story of repression and cure that is entirely directed toward the past. That is to say, it leaves out of account not only the cultural discourses that frame the search for the forgotten past, but also the analytical dialogue itself. Or rather, it "treats that dialogue as though . . . it is merely the shovel used to dig up history and so is of no account, except perhaps in manuals on the technique of digging up true chronologies."[39] The analogy between psychoanalysis and archaeology carries the assumption that "interpreted events are also original events."[40]

Within the framework of this story of repression and cure, the analogy with archaeology furthermore provides an explanation of the two components of reading in psychoanalysis: interpretation, or better, deciphering or decoding (*Deutung*), and (re)construction. As Jürgen Habermas has pointed out, Freud "patterned the interpretation of dreams after the hermeneutic model of philological research."[41] But, in so doing, he grafted philology onto archaeology. A passage, also cited previously, reads:

If his [the archaeologist's] work is crowned with success, the discoveries are self-explanatory: the ruined walls are part of the ramparts of a palace or a treasure-house; the fragments of columns can be filled out into a temple; *the numerous inscriptions, which, by good luck, may be bilingual, reveal an alphabet and a language, and, when they have been deciphered and translated, yield undreamed-of information about the events of the remote past.*[42]

The image of the bilingual inscription should, I think, be read as a prefiguration of Freud's distinction, in *The Interpretation of Dreams*, between the manifest and the latent dream. Introducing a new field of study, namely the dream work, he writes,

We are thus presented with a new task which had no previous existence: the task, that is, of investigating the relations between the manifest content of dreams and the latent dream-thoughts, and of tracing out the processes by which the latter have been changed into the former.

The dream-thoughts and the dream-content are presented to us like two versions of the same subject-matter [*desselben Inhaltes*] in two different languages. Or, more properly, the dream-content seems like a transcript of the dream-thoughts into another mode of expression, whose characters and syntactic laws it is our business to discover by comparing the original and the translation. The dream-thoughts are immediately comprehensible, as soon as we have learnt them. The dream-content, on the other hand, is expressed as it were in a pictographic script [*Bilderschrift*], the characters of which have to be transposed individually into the language of the dream-thoughts.[43]

The dream itself turns out to be a bilingual inscription; it presents us, Freud argues, with two different versions of the same psychic contents: one version, the latent dream, written in a language with which we are already familiar, and one, the manifest dream, given in an unknown and puzzling *Bilderschrift* analogous, for example, to Babylonian-Assyrian cuneiform or Egyptian hieroglyphs. In fact, this analogy has been suggested by Freud himself: "The interpretation of dreams," he says in *The Claims of Psycho-Analysis to Scientific Interest*, "is completely analogous to the decipherment of an ancient pictographic script such as Egyptian hieroglyphs."[44]

Thus the dream is represented by (nonphonetic) writing, by a written text. And, as is so often the case in Freud's work, writing or textuality implies indeterminacy. The work of deciphering is beset with all kinds of difficulties. We are told that the interpretation of dreams cannot be reduced to a simple one-to-one, sign-to-sign, decoding. There is no fixed key; psychoanalytic interpretation of dreams is not patterned upon popular "dream-books."[45] The notion of the dream as a hieroglyphic text emphasizes the radical ambiguity of the dream: "All such primitive systems of expression . . . are characterized by indefiniteness and ambiguity. . . . The coalescence of contraries in the dream-work is, as you know, analogous to the so-called 'antithetical meaning of primal words' in the most ancient languages."[46] It may even suggest the utter unreadability of the dream: "In these circumstances, you will conclude, so much room is left to the interpreter's arbitrary decision as to be incompatible with objective certainty in the findings" (p. 228).

Once again, however, the advances of modern archaeological science are called upon to confirm not only the readability of the dream, but also the objectivity of psychoanalytic deciphering. Archaeology provides an escape from ambiguity and indeterminacy. The passages quoted above conclude as follows:

> The lay public, including the scientific lay public, are well known to enjoy making a parade of scepticism when faced by the difficulties and uncertainties of a scientific achievement. I think they are wrong in this. You are perhaps not all aware that a similar situation arose in the history of the deciphering of the Babylonian-Assyrian inscriptions. There was a time when public opinion was very much inclined to regard the decipherers of cuneiform as visionaries and the whole of their researches as a "swindle." But in 1857 the Royal Asiatic Society made a decisive experiment. It requested four of the most highly respected experts in cuneiform, Rawlinson, Hincks, Fox Talbot, and Oppert, to send in, in sealed envelopes, independent translations of a newly discovered inscription; and, after a comparison between the four productions, it was able to announce that the agreement between these experts went far enough to justify a belief in what had so far been achieved and confidence in further advances. The derision on the part of the learned lay world gradually diminished after this, and since then certainty in reading cuneiform documents has increased enormously. (p. 232)

Embedded within the more comprehensive narrative of burial-and-excavation, the analogy with the bilingual document tells a story that is homologous to this "master-plot,"[47] namely, that dream interpretation is the bringing to light of an original mental content that has merely been disguised and concealed through the dream work. The path that leads to the formation of the dream is described as a regressive movement: due to the workings of censorship, the latent dream thoughts are driven back into the unconscious system and are here subjected to the dream work; the dream thoughts are transcribed into archaic, "hieroglyphic," characters. By asserting that the dream work is a transcription or translation of the latent dream into a piece of pictographic writing, Freud claims that the two texts, the latent and the manifest—or, to use his own suggestive metaphors, the "original" and the "translation"—are in fact identical, or rather that they express the same content.

The analyst's interpretation, accordingly, is represented as a retranslation of the manifest dream. The interpretation undoes the dream work and traces the manifest dream back to its original, the latent dream. As regards the dream theory, it seems obvious that the analogy with the bilingual document and its derivatives, the metaphors of "translation" and "original," did not merely serve to illustrate the psychoanalytic distinction between manifest and latent dream. On the contrary, the metaphors and analogies that relate to the bilingual inscription and to the deciphering of ancient scripts engendered the concept of the latent dream as a preexisting original which, through the dream work, is translated into the manifest hieroglyphic dream, but which may in turn be restored through the analyst's deciphering. The analogy with the bilingual inscription, then, tallies with the analogy with the archaeological excavation. Both tell the same story: interpreted events are also original events; interpreted dreams are also original dreams. Thus in the case of *The Interpretation of Dreams* it is an important point that Freud's terminology (latent/manifest dream, original/translation) does not allow any distinction between, on the one hand, the "dream-text" produced in the course of the dream interpretation and, on the other hand, the latent "dream-text" in which the manifest dream is supposed to originate.

In Chapter 1 we have seen how "Constructions in Analysis" seeks to situate the analytical construction, represented as the attempt "to reconstruct by means of supplementing and combining the surviving remains" (p. 259), within the archaeological model of psychoanalysis. However, before turning to this essay, let us first take another look at *Studies on Hysteria*. In connection with the case stories presented in this work, Freud has described the method of psychoanalysis as the procedure of clearing away pathogenic material, layer by layer, and has compared this procedure with the technique of excavating a buried city. In the last chapter, however, he arrives at a more complex definition of the work of analysis. While retaining the notion of the preservation of the past, as well as the idea of the spatial (layered) organization of the psychogenic material, he points out that this material can only enter consciousness piece by piece or fragment by fragment, as a stream of disconnected memories. The "pathogenic psychical material which has ostensibly been forgotten . . . in some fashion lies ready to hand and in correct and proper order" (p. 287), but only "a single memory at a time can enter ego-consciousness" (p. 291). The archaeological metaphor is momentarily abandoned in favor of another analogy, which, however, may be read as a prefiguration of the analogy between archaeological reconstructions and analytical constructions:

> The whole spatially-extended mass of psychogenic material is in this way drawn through a narrow cleft and thus arrives in consciousness cut up, as it were, into pieces or strips. It is the psychotherapist's business to put these together once more into the organization which he presumes to have existed. Anyone who has a craving for further similes may think at this point of a Chinese puzzle. (p. 291)

Almost thirty years later, in "Remarks on the Theory and Practice of Dream-Interpretation," the analogy with the jigsaw puzzle reappears—this time in connection with the problem of analytical constructions or, more precisely, with the problem of confirming and verifying these constructions. Freud writes:

> What makes him [the analyst] certain in the end is precisely the complication of the problem before him, which is like the solution of a jig-saw puzzle. A coloured picture, pasted upon a thin sheet of wood and fitting exactly into a wooden frame, is cut into a large number of pieces of the most irregular and crooked shapes. If one succeeds in arranging the confused heap of fragments, each of which bears upon it an unintelligible piece of drawing, so that the picture acquires a meaning, so that there is no gap anywhere in the design and so that the whole fits into the frame—if all these conditions are fulfilled, then one knows that one has solved the puzzle and that there is no alternative solution.[48]

And now the analogy, from "Constructions in Analysis," between the analytical construction and the archaeological restoration of an ancient dwelling place:

> But just as the archaeologist builds up the walls of the building from the foundations that have remained standing, determines the number and position of the columns from depressions in the

floor and reconstructs the mural decorations and paintings from the remains found in the débris, so does the analyst proceed when he draws his inferences from the fragments of memories, from the associations and from the behavior of the subject of the analysis. Both of them have an undisputed right to reconstruct by means of supplementing and combining the surviving remains. (p. 259)

Thus the analogy with the jigsaw puzzle and the analogy with the archaeological reconstruction both represent the analytical construction as the act of arranging and combining pieces or fragments, as the restoration of an original totality (a picture, an ancient dwelling place) that has been destroyed or cut into pieces. Indeed, the two analogies are identical, except for the fact that the analogy with archaeology takes into account the possibility that certain pieces are missing and therefore must be supplied by the analyst.[49]

Taken together, the two analogies support important assumptions concerning the object, the purpose, and the truth-value of analytical constructions. First, the analyst's work of construction is justified or authorized by the assumption of an existence of an original pattern or design, the existence of a complete "set of determinants" that is in itself coherent and meaningful and which may be reestablished. In order to assemble a puzzle, one must perceive "the confused heap of fragments" as parts of a consistent whole; in order to carry on an archaeological reconstruction, one must see "the remains found in the debris" as fragments of an ancient edifice. It follows by extension that the analyst, in order to construct, must see the material produced in analysis as parts of a singular pattern. To construct is to assemble these parts, to put the fragments "together once more into the organization which [the analyst] presumes to have existed." The correct construction, consequently, is that which faithfully restores the original design.

Second, design—or "meaning"—is supposed to emerge from the fragments; the solution, as it were, lies in the material the analyst brings to light. The fit of the fragments is in itself the confirmation of the (re)construction. The correctness of nonauthentic, reconstructed pieces is determined by the context, by the surrounding fragments; the extent to which they fit in with or are consistent with original pieces becomes an indication of their correctness. If the analyst succeeds in arranging the parts so that the design is meaningful and complete, he has succeeded in restoring the organization that once existed. And further, he has arrived at a solution that excludes alternative ways of organizing the excavated material. The analogy with the jigsaw puzzle and the analogy with the archaeological reconstruction both support the assumption of the "singularity of meaning"[50] or the "axiom of the singular solution."[51]

In light of the preceding pages, *Gradiva* (as interpreted by Freud) reads as an analogy of the analogy with archaeology. If psychoanalysis and archaeology, as Freud assumes, may reflect each other, then Jensen's "Pompeian Fantasy" is a mirror that reflects the similarities between the two fields of study, the parallels between the individual's repressed past and the buried remains of an ancient culture and between the psychoanalytic process and the archaeologist's excavation and reconstruction. Another, and perhaps more adequate, definition of the place of *Gradiva* in psychoanalysis would be to speak of Jensen's story as the exemplary archaeological account of psychoanalysis. Jensen has unfolded the narrative implicit in Freud's analogy with archaeology and given it the form of a short novel. *Gradiva* is a psychoanalytic narrative of burial and excavation—a narrative that brings together all the issues I have touched on above: repression, symptom formation, and dreams, as well as dream interpretation and (re)construction in analysis. According to Freud's reading, Jensen's protagonist has not simply "forgotten" his childhood sweetheart; he has repressed the memory of Zoe together with his own sexuality, and his fantasies about Gradiva are therefore to be seen as symptoms, as "derivatives of his repressed memories" of his childhood friendship with Zoe Bertgang. It seems that the author has intuitively grasped the connection between such a repression of a childhood memory and the burial of Pompeii. His novel is built on two opposite movements: Norbert Hanold's forgetting of his childhood friend, dramatized as Zoe Bertgang's "burial" and her metamorphosis into an ancient artifact, and the dismantling of Norbert's delusion, that is, his retrieval of Zoe among the ruins of Pompeii—the metamorphosis of Gradiva into Zoe. Thus the fates of the two main characters are inextricably bound up with that of the ancient city.

While Norbert Hanold is still back in Germany, trying to reconstruct the life of the model of the Gradiva relief, he has a peculiar dream. In the dream, the young archaeologist finds himself in Pompeii. The year is A.D. 79, and it is the very day of the fatal eruption of Vesuvius. The volcano colors the sky burning red, and the air is heavy with sulphur. Suddenly Norbert catches sight of Gradiva (he recognizes her characteristic gait), who is on her way to the temple of Apollo. Till then he has had no thought of her presence, but now it seems natural that Gradiva, since she is a Pompeian, is an inhabitant of the dying town and that she thus "without his having any suspicion of it, was his contemporary." The archaeologist, all of a sudden foreseeing the young woman's destiny, calls out. But Gradiva just stares blankly at him and then proceeds to the temple that is to become her grave:

> At the same time, her face became paler as if it were changing to white marble; she stepped up to the portico of the Temple, and then, between the pillars, she sat down on a step and slowly laid her head upon it. Now the pebbles were falling in such masses that they condensed into a completely opaque curtain; hastening quickly after her, however, he found his way to the place where she had disappeared from his view, and there she lay, protected by the projecting roof, stretched out on the broad step, as if for sleep, but no longer breathing, apparently stifled by the sulphur fumes. From Vesuvius the red glow flared over her countenance, which, with closed eyes, was exactly like that of a beautiful statue.[52]

The living Gradiva is gradually transformed into a stone sculpture that is buried under masses of lava. This dream, Freud comments, is "no more than an ingenious and poetical representation of the real event" (p. 60); had the young archaeologist been able to read it, it would have provided him with a clue, not only to the cause of his obsession with the Gradiva relief, but also to the real identity of Gradiva: she is his "contemporary"; they live in the same town. Indeed, Norbert Hanold's Pompeian dream appears to provide him with a precise account of what really happened: in repressing the memory of Zoe, Norbert has "buried" her and transferred or displaced his libidinous attachment from the living girl to an archaeological object, the ancient relief. When Norbert imagines Gradiva to be an inhabitant of classical Pompeii, he is, therefore, in a certain way quite right, because, says Freud,

> no other or better analogy could be found in his science for his remarkable state, in which he became aware of his memories of his childhood friendship through obscure channels of information. Once he had made his own childhood coincide with the classical past (which it was so easy for him to do), there was a perfect similarity between the burial of Pompeii—the disappearance of the past combined with its preservation—and repression. (p. 51)

The author was well justified, indeed, in lingering over the valuable similarity which his delicate sense had perceived between a

particular mental process in the individual and an isolated historical event in the history of mankind. (p. 40)

Norbert Hanold literally recovers "his" Gradiva among the excavated temples and houses of Pompeii, but he finds her as a ghost.
Ghost means death. Accordingly, the young archaeologist presents the
woman, whom he thinks has returned from the land of the dead, with
an asphodel, the white flower of the underworld. Yet, in doing so,
Norbert expresses the wish that Gradiva "lived" and "still existed."
Indeed, the meetings between Norbert and Gradiva are ambiguously
suspended between death and life; Gradiva-the-ghost is, as it were, an
intermediary between the antique relief into which Norbert has turned
Zoe and the living woman she is about to become. The meetings
provide two climactic scenes. First, Norbert touches the hand of Gradiva; it is the warm hand of a living human being. Just then Gradiva is
addressed as "Zoe" (Greek for "Life"). Norbert flees; significantly, he
runs toward "the Street of the Tombs." But Zoe follows and among the
ruins of the Villa of Diomedes the second scene takes place. As Zoe
brings out Norbert's forgotten, repressed childhood, the young archaeologist is finally set free from his delusion; explanation and cure
coincide. Referring to herself as "something excavated and restored to
life,"[53] Zoe seals her own transformation back into a contemporary
woman of flesh and blood.

From a Freudian point of view, *Gradiva* appears to be a kind of
psychodrama featuring three main personae, namely, the patient, his
repressed love object, and the analyst who cures him; Zoe, of course,
plays the role of love object and the role of analyst. Referring to Zoe as
"physician" or "therapist" (pp. 87, 88), Freud carefully emphasizes that
her treatment of her former playmate presents a correct image of the
psychoanalytic process. "The procedure which the author makes his
Zoe adopt for curing her childhood friend's delusion shows a far-
reaching similarity—no, a complete agreement in its essence—with a
therapeutic method which was introduced into medical practice in
1895 by Dr. Josef Breuer and myself" (pp. 88–89). Zoe cleverly sees
through Norbert's delusion, and gradually she discovers the connection between his present state of mind and the events of the forgotten
past. Concealing and yet revealing her own true identity, Zoe step by
step leads her friend toward recovery—the recovery that is achieved as
she, in the form of a story in the story, presents Norbert with a reconstruction of his forgotten years. Zoe, writes Freud, gives her friend back
"from outside the repressed memories which he could not set free
from inside" (p. 88).

From the perspective of the analogy between psychoanalysis and archaeology, Zoe thus plays the role of the archaeologist. And, indeed, *Gradiva* suggests that she, quite literally, becomes a kind of archaeologist. While excavating her friend's inner Pompeii, Zoe, at the same time, displays an archaeological knowledge that surpasses that of the deluded archaeologist. At the time when Norbert is still caught in the web of delusion, he buys a brooch he believes to be an antiquity, a grave find from ancient Pompeii. The brooch is obviously a modern imitation, a mere souvenir, but Norbert, having apparently forgotten his archaeological learning, firmly believes that it once belonged to Gradiva. Zoe, however, is not deceived: "He searched in his breast pocket and added, as he drew out the object, 'Has this brooch ever belonged to you?' She leaned forward a little toward it, but shook her head, 'No, I can't remember. Chronologically it would, of course, not be impossible, for it probably did not exist until this year.' "[54] Thus Zoe provides the link between the work of the analyst and the work of the archaeologist. Toward the end of the story she, significantly, describes her therapeutical treatment of Norbert in archaeological terms. Referring to the retrieval of her childhood friend, she exclaims: "I said to myself that I should certainly dig up something interesting alone here. Of course I had not reckoned at all on the find which I made."[55]

At this point, however, the novel has become both more complicated and more simple than the analogy it is called upon to support. *Gradiva* presents us with an archaeologist (Norbert Hanold) who is unaware of and unable to excavate his own inner Pompeii, and an archaeological find (Zoe Bertgang), who is at the same time the (psycho)archaeologist who uncovers the friend of her childhood. The archaeologist is the thing to be excavated—and vice versa. Later in this study I return to *Gradiva,* and to Freud's reading of the story, in order to show how Zoe's double role may ultimately undermine the analogy with archaeology Jensen's novel is called upon to support. For the time being, let it remain unequivocal that the author of *Gradiva,* by assigning to Zoe the double role of grave find and archaeologist, seems to grasp the very essence of Freud's analogy with archaeology: the axiom that interpreted or (re)constructed events are also original events. By being herself the grave find she excavates, Zoe guarantees the truth of the past she brings to light. Jensen seems to have endowed his heroine with absolute authority; she has that which the analyst would have liked to have, namely, a privileged access to the buried past.

By pointing to the grave finds that adorned his consulting rooms, Freud stated that the past is preserved internally like buried antiquities and consequently may be recovered through analytical excavation. By pointing to Jensen's *Gradiva* as the ally of psychoanalysis, he confirmed his own narrative of psychoanalysis as an archaeology of the soul. The relationship in *Gradiva* between repression and burial and between therapy and excavation made it possible for Freud to read Jensen's novel as a connecting link between psychoanalysis and archaeology, or as trope of his own master trope. Considering the task Jensen's novel was called upon to perform, it is not surprising to learn that Gradiva finally was added to Freud's collection of antiquities. Having finished *Delusions and Dreams in Jensen's* Gradiva, Freud bought a cast of the "Gradiva" relief (the original is owned by the Vatican Museum), which he placed in his consulting room along with his Greek, Egyptian, and Roman antiquities. And thereafter "it became fashionable among analysts to have a copy of the relief on their walls."[56] Gradiva had become an emblem of psychoanalysis.

Chapter 3

Construction in the Case of the Wolf Man

Donald M. Kartiganer has suggested that Freud's famous case story of the Wolf Man, published under the title *From the History of an Infantile Neurosis*, should be read as a story of reading in psychoanalysis. The case of the Wolf Man "is the most comprehensive account we have of [Freud's] interpretative procedure." Its "primary value for us as literary critics lies in its detailed demonstration of Freud as reader." The case history, Kartiganer continues, constitutes "an implicit hermeneutics and a practical criticism, a theory of how to read and a detailed demonstration of how reading proceeds."[1] As stories of reading in psychoanalysis, *From the History of an Infantile Neurosis* and *Delusions and Dreams in Jensen's* Gradiva may be juxtaposed. This I will do in the following chapter, as I present Freud's analysis of the Wolf Man as a "counterstory" to his reading of *Gradiva* that takes the novel to be the emblematic story of psychoanalysis-as-archaeology.

Set against *Gradiva*'s simplified model of the psychoanalytic process as an archaeological excavation and reconstruction of the past, *From the History of an Infantile Neurosis* marks a new questioning (which, however, folds back on previous discussions) of how the object of the psychoanalytic quest, the patient's forgotten past, is related to the analytical process itself. Peter Brooks has said that Freud, in the case of the Wolf Man, discovers "'detection' and its narrative to be extraordinarily more complex and problematic . . . and indeed inextricably bound up with the fictional."[2] In fact, the problem of fictionality presents itself very directly to Freud in the form of the unverifiable "primal scene," the analytic construction around which the entire analysis revolves. Thus the case story, ironically enough, reintroduces the question of fiction and fictionality that Freud has neglected by reading Jensen's "Fantasy" as a psychiatric study.

However, if the analysis of the Wolf Man embraces the problem of fictionality, it is not because Freud adopts a Spencian model of psycho-analytic interpretation as an "aesthetic experience" and renounces his quest for lost origins. On the contrary, *From the History of an Infantile Neurosis*—which was written as a contribution to the dispute with Jung and Adler concerning "the significance of the infantile factor"[3]—constitutes perhaps Freud's most ambitious attempt to descend "into the deepest and most primitive strata of mental development" (p. 10). What Freud will come to realize is, however, that such a descent in search of lost origins necessarily takes the analyst into the realm of "*as though*" (p. 50; Freud's italics). The "infantile factor" that is the object of the analyst's quest only presents itself as the "primal scene"—the constructed scene, which (as Ned Lukacher has it in an interesting study of the primal scene in psychoanalysis) becomes a figure for "the crisis of interpretation that emerges when the question of the origin becomes at once unavoidable and unanswerable, when the origin must be remembered but memory fails utterly, when all the evidence points towards an origin that nevertheless remains unverifiable."[4]

From the History of an Infantile Neurosis has over the years been the subject of various readings and discussions emphasizing different aspects of this complex and highly suggestive text.[5] My own reading is first of all indebted to the works of those critics and theorists who inquire into the mechanism of *deferred action* on which the entire case hinges, most notably to Jean Laplanche's brilliant close readings.[6] It was in the nineties that Freud introduced the concept of deferred action—or *Nachträglichkeit*, as it should properly be called, since the term designates not only a belated or postponed reaction, but a supplementary action.[7] As Laplanche's lucid commentaries have made clear, *Nachträglichkeit* is a figure for temporal spacing that challenges the spatiotemporal model of the mind, derived from archaeology, as it compels a revision of the theorem of the timelessness of the unconscious.

What Laplanche's treatment does not sufficiently examine are the ways in which the logic of deferred action, in the case of the Wolf Man, is brought to bear on the concept of construction in analysis. Freud's discussion of the epistemological status and the therapeutic effects of the unverifiable primal scene suggests that the mechanism of deferred action encompasses the analytical dialogue itself, and that the analytical construction is only comprehensible as an instance of *Nachträglichkeit*. By returning to the theory of deferred action and by applying this theory to the discussion of the analytical process, Freud has made a remarkable contribution to the understanding of the workings of the mind, as well as to the discussion of reading in psychoanalysis. The case of the Wolf Man invites us to conceive of *Nachträglichkeit*, not as an isolated phenomenon in the history of the formation of the neurosis, but as a general psychic—and textual—mechanism. Freud hereby presents us with an implicit theory of the dynamics of construction in analysis that is, by the same token, a theory of reading in psycho-analysis challenging the archaeological model of which *Gradiva* is the emblem.

The history of *From the History of an Infantile Neurosis* is itself a story of belatedness and deferral; it is the story of the deferred publication of an account of a treatment, written with some delay, of a neurosis analyzed fifteen years after the fact. The Wolf Man was twenty-three years old when, in 1910, he began the analysis with Freud that was to last until July 1914. Freud began writing the case story a few months later, but four years elapsed before it was published in 1918. The temporal gap between the completion of the analysis and the publica-tion of the case history proved to be significant, for Freud interspersed his account of the case with important commentaries that throw new light on his analysis. As one critic has remarked, the text, as it appears in *The Standard Edition,* reads like a palimpsest, with new interpreta-tions inscribed on top of, but not effacing, previous interpretations.[8]

In fact, Freud never got finished with this case. The case of the Wolf Man, which recapitulates discussion dating from the very first psychoanalytic publications, returns to haunt one of his very last es-says, "Analysis Terminable and Interminable" (1937).[9] Obviously, no single reading can do justice to all aspects of this rich and complex case. My discussion of construction in the case of the Wolf Man takes as its point of departure Freud's interpretation of the wolf dream—the dream that marks the onset of the patient's infantile neurosis "which began immediately before his fourth birthday as an anxiety-hysteria (in the shape of an animal phobia), then changed into an obsessional neurosis with a religious content, and lasted with its offshoots as far as into his tenth year" (p. 8). I shall then proceed to Freud's discussion of the primal scene in the fifth chapter, the last part of which was added immediately before the publication of the case in 1918, and finally to his reading of the Grusha scene.

On the night before his fourth birthday, the child had a dream from which he awoke in a state of extreme anxiety. Almost twenty years later, the Wolf Man, in his analysis with Freud, reproduced the dream as follows:

> *"I dreamt that it was night and that I was lying in my bed. (My bed stood with its foot towards the window; in front of the window there was a row of old walnut trees. I know it was winter when I had the dream, and night-*

time.) Suddenly the window opened of its own accord, and I was terrified to see that some white wolves were sitting on the big walnut tree in front of the window. There were six or seven of them. The wolves were quite white, and looked more like foxes or sheep-dogs, for they had big tails like foxes and they had their ears pricked like dogs when they pay attention to something. In great terror, evidently of being eaten up by the wolves, I screamed and woke up." (p. 29; Freud's italics)

This dream, which marked the beginning of the child's animal phobia, was related at an early stage of the analysis, but the interpretation dragged on over several years, says Freud, and "it was only during the last months of the analysis that it became possible to understand it completely" (p. 33).

In an essay published in 1913, Freud had commented on those features of this dream that derive from fairy tales.[10] The Wolf Man related that he, as a small child, had suffered from a fear of an illustration in a picture book of a wolf, "standing upright" (p. 16). Whenever he saw this picture he would start screaming for fear that the wolf should come and "eat him up." His older sister enjoyed tormenting him with this particular book. He himself tried to avoid it, but she always succeeded in arranging things so that he was obliged to look at the picture. The dream was related to this picture book, which the Wolf Man later identified as the story of "The Wolf and the Seven Little Goats." In the course of the analysis, the patient further associated it with other fairy tales, in particular one he had heard his grandfather tell, and which ran as follows: A tailor was sitting in a room, when the window opened and a wolf leapt in. The tailor caught the wolf by its tail and pulled it off. Some time later the tailor was walking in the forest and suddenly saw a pack of wolves coming toward him. In order to escape from them, he climbed into a tree. But the tailless wolf, which was among them, proposed that they should climb, one upon another, till the last one could reach him. In 1913 Freud had merely concluded that the wolf was "a first father-surrogate" (p. 32); the fear the wolf excited did in fact pertain to the child's relationship with his father. *From the History of an Infantile Neurosis* does not stop here, but claims that the dream must have been preceded by some "unknown scene" (p. 33) that had the following characteristics: *"A real occurrence—dating from a very early period—looking—immobility—sexual problems—castration—his father—something terrible"* (p. 34; Freud's italics).

In his analysis Freud had pursued, without apparent success, the theme of castration the fairy tales dramatize. But suddenly "the patient . . . called to mind the fact that, when he was still very small, 'on the first estate,' his sister has seduced him into sexual practices" (p. 20).

The boy reacted to this seduction by trying in turn to seduce his beloved nurse: he began to masturbate in her presence. The nurse, however, answered with a threat, "she made a serious face, and explained that that wasn't good; children who did that, she added, got a 'wound' in the place" (p. 24). This piece of information gave rise to further sexual inquiries; the boy began to ponder the differences between the sexes and the theme of castration. But, Freud points out, although the child was occupied with thoughts of castration, he at that time had no belief in it and no dread of it. The nurse's rejection, however, had a further consequence. Soon after the castration threat the boy gave up masturbation and regressed to an earlier psychosexual phase. "His sexual life . . . which was beginning to come under the sway of the genital zone, gave way before an external obstacle, and was thrown back by its influence into an earlier phase of pregenital organization" (p. 25). The boy indulged in fantasies of cruelty against animals, but eventually these sadist impulses were turned against his own person. The seduction, Freud concludes, had forced the boy into a passive sexual role that would determine his relationship with his father. After having been rejected by his Nanya, the child turned to his father, trying to obtain a masochistic, anal gratification through physical punishment.

It is this story of the boy's sexual development before the dream that "makes it possible for us to fill in the gaps in the dream" (p. 35). *The Interpretation of Dreams* has established that dreams are wish fulfillments. The wish concerned in the formation of the wolf dream, reasons Freud, must have been the wish for the sexual satisfaction the child was at that time longing to obtain from his father. "The strength of the wish made it possible to revive a long-forgotten trace in his memory of a scene which was able to show him what sexual satisfaction from his father was like; and the result was terror, horror of the fulfillment of the wish" (pp. 35–36). It follows that the "unknown scene" that forms the object of the analyst's quest must, above all, satisfy one condition: in order to account for the anxiety the wish fulfillment provoked, it must have been an event able to "create a conviction of the reality of the existence of castration" (p. 36).

"I have now reached the point at which I must abandon the support I have hitherto had from the course of the analysis. I am afraid it will also be the point at which the reader's belief will abandon me" (p. 36). With these words Freud begins his account of the unknown scene behind the wolf dream. What "sprang into activity" that night was nothing but the memory of a scene that took place one afternoon when the child, aged one and a half years, was in bed in his parents' room, suffering from a fit of malaria.

He had been sleeping in his cot, then, in his parents' bedroom, and woke up, perhaps because of his rising fever, in the afternoon, possibly at five o'clock, the hour which was later marked out by depression. It harmonizes with our assumption that it was a hot summer's day, if we suppose that his parents had retired, half undressed, for an afternoon *siesta.* When he woke up, he witnessed a coitus *a tergo,* three times repeated; he was able to see his mother's genitals as well as his father's organ; and he understood the process as well as its significance. (p. 37)

A comparison between this primal scene and the wolf dream thus reveals significant transformations. During the primal scene the boy passively watched his mother and father dressed in white underwear (the latter assumed the same posture as the upright wolf in the picture book). In the dream the white wolves are watching *him* in a very threatening way. According to Freud, this reversal indicates that the dream activated the memory of the coitus scene, but gave it a new and frightening meaning: "If you want to be sexually satisfied by Father . . . you must allow yourself to be castrated like Mother" (p. 47). By way of the anxiety dream, the primal scene had thus become the ultimate proof of the reality of castration.

How does Freud arrive at this reconstruction of the event that supposedly underlies the patient's wolf dream? What are the circumstances under which it is produced in the analysis? We do not know. Indeed, his admittance of the fact that the primal scene is "the point at which the reader's belief will abandon me" is almost too convenient, insofar as it seems to exempt him from going into details concerning the emergence of the primal scene. Who suggested it? Should we think of it as the return in analysis of a repressed childhood memory? Having discussed its plausibility, Freud, in passing, refers to the event as "the *constructed* primal scene" (p. 39; my italics). However, it is only the following chapter ("A Few Discussions") that provides us with more information as to the status of the scene. The account of the Wolf Man's experience of watching his parents' intercourse is here explicitly designated as the analyst's construction: "So far as my experience hitherto goes, these scenes from infancy are not reproduced during the treatment as recollections, they are products of construction" (p. 50). And, Freud continues:

scenes, like this one in my present patient's case, which date from such an early period and exhibit a similar content, and which further lay claim to such an extraordinary significance for the history of the case, are as a rule not reproduced as recollections, but have to be divined—constructed—gradually and laboriously from an aggregate of indications. (p. 51)

Thus the primal scene at the heart of the Wolf Man's infantile neurosis is the one thing that is *not* reproduced as a memory in analysis—and which is at no point actually verified through the patient's recollections. The entire case story therefore depends upon a hypothetical construction that cannot be replaced by an authentic recollection. Freud's analysis revolves around an absence, a void, that can only be filled with a construction emerging from the analytical dialogue.

In his papers on technique Freud several times brings up the problems of verification these constructed scenes of early childhood pose. Why does not the "path that starts from the analyst's construction . . . end in the patient's recollection" of the event?[11] In "Remarks on the Theory and Practice of Dream Interpretation" he suggests that the impossibility of verifying constructions like the Wolf Man's primal scene may be due to the fact that, strictly speaking, there is nothing to remember. The decisive scene may not be an event but an unconscious fantasy—something that never happened and therefore cannot be remembered. "What we are dealing with," he writes, "may not be the reproduction of a real and forgotten event but the bringing forward of an unconscious phantasy, about which no feeling of memory is ever to be expected."[12]

This assumption echoes "Remembering, Repeating and Working-Through" which was published in 1914, the year Freud terminated his analysis of the Wolf Man. This essay once again raises the important issue of infantile amnesia. As a rule, it is maintained, everything that has been forgotten is still present and may be recuperated. But after having asserted that a total abolition of infantile amnesia is indeed possible, he goes on to discuss two important exceptions from this rule. First of all, fantasies, emotional impulses, and thought connections must, in their relation to memory, be considered separately from memories of real events and experiences. As to fantasies and emotional impulses, "it particularly often happens that something is 'remembered' which could never have been 'forgotten' because it was never at any time noticed—was never conscious."[13]

The wording "was never conscious" points toward Freud's metapsychological investigation from 1915, "Repression." In order to account for repression, one must, says Freud, assume the existence of a "primal repression," which "consists in the psychical (ideational) representative of the instinct being denied entrance into the consciousness." Primal repression is that which logically and ontologically precedes repression proper, which Freud accordingly defines as "an after-pressure."[14] Repression is thus always already anticipated by repression, by a mythical moment of original repression that constitutes the condition of possibility of repression proper, but which can only be hypothetically deduced from the phenomenon of after-pressure.

The implication is that the core of the unconscious is made up of primal representations that, by definition, have never been conscious. It follows that these representations can never be reproduced as recollections; the core of the unconscious is, as Serge Viderman points out, only knowable through "les 'constructions' simplement probables de l'analyste."[15] But, claims Freud in "Remembering, Repeating and Working-Through," the "conviction which the patient obtains in the course of his analysis" of the truthfulness of such constructions is "quite independent of this kind of memory" (p. 149). This, too, applies to the analyst's constructions of those experiences that constitute Freud's second example: a "special class of experiences of the utmost importance for which no memory can as a rule be recovered. These are experiences which occurred in very early childhood and were not understood at the time but which were *subsequently* [*nachträglich*] understood and interpreted." The patient, he continues, "after his resistances have been overcome, no longer invokes the absence of any memory . . . as a ground for refusing to accept them" (p. 149). Writing these lines, Freud, in fact, had the case of the Wolf Man in mind.

The reflections on fantasy, event, and memory in "Remarks on the Theory and Practice of Dream Interpretation" and in "Remembering, Repeating and Working-Through" bring us to the crucial discussion, in the fifth chapter of *From the History of an Infantile Neurosis*, of the status of the primal scene. Freud here suggests two alternative readings of the constructed scene, which he attempts to position within the patient's prehistory: The scene may be seen as an unconscious fantasy, something that never really happened and therefore could not be remembered. Or it may be regarded as a real event—but an event that only became meaningful to the child through subsequent interpretation.

Following Freud, let us initially adopt a provisional belief in the reality of the primal scene: the analytical construction has captured an original happening; the boy did actually, around the age of eighteen months, witness his parents' intercourse a tergo. Simple as it may seem, this hypothesis in fact queries the archaeological model of psychoanalysis. The assumption of the reality of the primal scene entails a new questioning of how cause and effect, "early" and "late," are related. The regressive analytical movement—the procedure that has elsewhere been described as a process of "clearing away the pathogenic psychical material layer by layer"—has revealed a scene from "the prehistoric period of childhood" (p. 18), but a scene that in itself had no original meaning or impact. "Tracing a hysterical symptom back to a traumatic scene," Freud pointed out in one of his early papers, "assists our understanding only if the scene satisfies two conditions; if it possesses the relevant *suitability to serve as a determinant* and if it recognizably possesses the necessary *traumatic force*."[16] While the Wolf Man's primal scene appears to satisfy the first condition, it does not seem to possess the necessary traumatic force—at least it was not (in Freud's terminology) "effective," that is, it had no immediate traumatizing effect.

Thus the hypothesis of the primal scene's authenticity suggests that the material brought out during the analysis combines in two quite different patterns or sequences: one that is chronological (the child's observation of the primal scene around the age of one and a half years, the seduction by his sister dated to the age of three and a quarter, the anxiety dream right before his fourth birthday), and one that pertains to the formation and outbreak of the neurosis. According to the latter, the wolf dream's reactivation of the primal scene, rather than the primal scene itself, has priority, since it marks the onset of the phobia. Commenting on the sexual development of the case, Freud remarks that this development "was *first* decisively influenced by the seduction, and was *then* diverted by the scene of the observation of the coitus, *which in its deferred action operated like a second seduction*" (p. 47; my italics).

In his account of the primal scene, Freud has said that the child "witnessed a coitus *a tergo,* three times repeated; he was able to see his mother's genitals as well as his father's organ; and he understood the process as well as its significance." But in a footnote, he continues,

> I mean that he understood it at the time of the dream when he was four years old, not at the time of the observation. He received the impressions when he was one and a half; his understanding of them was deferred, but became possible at the time of the dream owing to his development, his sexual excitations, and his sexual researches. (pp. 37–38, note 6)

The archaeological model takes into account that the memory of a particular event can make its appearance in a psychological stratum where it does not belong. That is to say, the memory has been pushed backward or forward in time, and the analyst must therefore determine the actual age of the find and reestablish the correct chronology of events. Here Freud is not simply talking about forward or backward projection, or about a delayed reaction to what once happened. The point is that the primal scene in itself was void of meaning, or rather it was the space of various potential readings. It was thus the anxiety dream, at the age of four, that ascribed a horrifying meaning (the reality of castration) to that which happened that afternoon in the parents' bedroom. And this interpretation, as well as the pathological effects it provoked or produced, were only made possible by that which had later happened to the child: the sister's seduction, the nurse's threat of castration, his psychosexual development. It is only because of these incidents that the observation, which according to Freud articulates the essence of the child's psychic conflict, makes sense: "If you want to be sexually satisfied by Father, you must allow yourself to be castrated like Mother." The meaning and the impact of the primal scene were thus determined by subsequent material. His analysis has revealed an original traumatic scene from the primal period—but a scene that originally had no traumatic effect, a scene that became a trauma only after the fact, that is, by deferred action.

The alternative to this understanding of the Wolf Man's primal scene is, according to Freud, to regard it as an unconscious fantasy. That is to say, the scene is a fiction that has no material reality, but which nevertheless, for the subject, has the effect of reality and is able to provoke psychic disturbances. "The phantasies possess *psychical* as contrasted with *material* reality, and we gradually learn to understand that *in the world of the neuroses it is the psychical reality which is the decisive kind.*"[17] Still, the child must have seen or heard something, Freud goes on to say, since neither children nor adults are able to create fantasies out of nothing. However, what the boy saw might not have been his parents' intercourse but the copulation between dogs (the wolves in the dream resembled dogs). According to this, we have two scenes, both nontraumatic. First, the parents' afternoon siesta when the boy, aged one and a half, slept in their bedroom. "The child woke up from his sleep, but—the scene was innocent" (p. 58). Second, the copulation between dogs, which the child accidentally saw right before, or perhaps several months before, the wolf dream. The traumatic scene, then, is itself a fantasmatic construction.[18] The child fused the memory of the siesta with the image of copulating dogs and thus created the scene that in turn was projected back into his early childhood.

> What supervened during the expectant excitement of the night of this dream was the transference on to his parents of his recently acquired memory-picture, with *all* its details, and it was only thus that the powerful emotional effects which followed were made possible. He now arrived at a deferred understanding of the impressions which he may have received a few weeks or months earlier. (p. 58)

It was thus the dream, or more precisely the dream work, that accomplished the fusion of parents and dogs and *simultaneously* created the manifest dream (the wolf dream) as well as its latent content, the primal scene. The dream that appears to activate the memory of the infantile scene did in fact produce it. Again the notion of "the original" turns out to be extremely problematic. In fact, we are presented with a concept of the relationship between latent and manifest dream that stands at odds with what we have discussed above. Rather than being the preexisting original of the manifest dream (the "translation"), the latent dream appears to be the product of the dream work. The latent dream, then, is not a dream text concealed behind the manifest surface; it is rather the reverse side of this surface. Latent and manifest dream are as inseparable as are the two sides of a sheet of paper.

No doubt Freud would prefer to be able to present his constructed primal scene as an authentic happening; the case story, however, does not allow him to make a definite choice between fantasy and real event. Toward the end of chapter 5 Freud states that he intends "on this occasion to close the discussion of the reality of the primal scene with a *non liquet*" (p. 60). However, warning the reader that "the case history is not yet at an end" (p. 60), Freud postpones a final decision. When he later returns to the discussion of the status of the primal scene, however, the question of the reality of this scene is said to be of no great importance. "I should myself be glad to know whether the primal scene in my present patient's case was a phantasy or a real experience; but . . . I must admit that the answer to this question is not in fact a matter of very great importance" (p. 97). Instead he stresses the fact that the patient has acquired a profound conviction of the reality of the primal scene, and that fantasies just as well as real events are able to produce pathogenic effects. "It remains a fact that the patient has created these phantasies for himself," he writes in *Introductory Lectures on Psycho-Analysis,* "and this fact is of scarcely less importance for his neurosis than if he had really experienced what the phantasies contain."[19]

The question of the status of the primal scene—real event or fantasy—and Freud's discussion of this problem have given rise to several commentaries, not only from psychoanalysts, but also from literary critics and theorists concerned with psychoanalysis and narrative. On the one hand, it is argued, the status of this scene is of no importance, since the effect is identical in both cases. Both versions "give us very similar narratives," claims Jonathan Culler:

> If one opts for the production of the event by forces of signification, it becomes clear that the primal fantasy, as we might call it, can be efficacious only if the imagined event functions for the

4-year-old as a real event from his past. And if, on the other hand, we opt for the reality of the primal scene, we can see that this event could not have had the disastrous consequences it did unless the structures of signification which made it a trauma for the Wolfman and gave it irresistible explanatory power were so suited to it as to make it in some sense necessary. The fact that the event supposedly experienced at age 1 1/2 became a trauma only through deferred action at age 4 shows the powerful role of the forces of meaning.[20]

And yet, on the other hand, it does make a difference whether the primal scene is construed as a real event or as a fantasy. And it is certainly of great importance that Freud refuses to chose between the two readings. *From the History of an Infantile Neurosis* presents us with possibly reversible chains of association, says Peter Brooks. "The relation between *fabula* and *sjuzet*, between event and its significant reworking, is one of suspicion and conjecture, a structure of indeterminacy which can offer only a framework of narrative possibilities rather than a clearly specifiable plot."[21] I shall come back to this discussion later. At this point, let me return to Freud's argument, which does not stop at the juxtaposition of two different readings.

As it turns out, the choice is not between two but *three* solutions. On the last pages of his case story, Freud offers yet another reading of the primal scene. According to the dog hypothesis, the primal scene is a fantasmatic creation based on actual observation. It may be that we do not need an observation of copulating dogs in order to explain the formation of the unconscious fantasy. The decisive factor may not in fact belong to the realm of individual experience.

This, at least, is the assumption that leads to the third solution, according to which the fantasy of the primal scene owes its existence to the interference of superindividual "schemata, which, like the categories of philosophy, are concerned with the business of 'placing' the impressions derived from actual experience" (p. 119). Freud advances this theory in *Introductory Lectures on Psycho-Analysis,* in the context of a discussion of the epistemological status of the cluster of recurring infantile fantasies that deal with the all-important question of origin: the fantasy of castration, which considers the origin of gender difference; the fantasy of seduction, which pertains to the question of the origin of sexuality; and, finally, the fantasy of the primal scene. It is suggested that the individual, in creating these *"primal phantasies,"* "reaches beyond his own experience into primaeval experience at points where his own experience has been too rudimentary." Children "in their phantasies are simply filling in the gaps in individual truth with prehistoric truth."[22] The schemata, continues Freud in the case of the Wolf Man, are to be seen as phylogenetically inherited precipitates from the history of human civilization.

> The Oedipus complex, which comprises a child's relation to his parents, is one of them—is, in fact, the best known member of the class. Wherever experiences fail to fit in with the hereditary schema, they become remodelled in the imagination—a process which might very profitably be followed out in detail. It is precisely such cases that are calculated to convince us of the independent existence of the schema. We are often able to see the schema triumphing over the experience of the individual. . . . The contradictions between experience and the schema seem to supply the conflicts of childhood with an abundance of material. (pp. 119–20)

The reference to phylogenetic inheritance may be read as a kind of concession to Jung's theory of the archetype. Perhaps, however, we do not need the (mythical) prehistory of mankind in order to explain the workings of the schemata. What puzzles Freud is the occurrence of certain infantile fantasies that differ very little from individual to individual, but which cannot, in each case, be explained as imprints of identical experiences. Apart from representing the schema as hereditary, Freud, in the paragraph cited above, characterizes it as follows: first, the schema is superindividual, in the sense that it exists prior to and independent of individual experience; second, experiences are "placed," that is, structured or organized, according to the schema; and, third, any discrepancy between schema and individual experience is able to produce a psychic conflict. The schema hypothesis, then, suggests the reality of a preexistant structure that informs phantasmal constructions. Laplanche and Pontalis suggest that this structure should be seen as a prefiguration of Lacan's "symbolic order":

> [I]f, beneath the diversity of individual fables, we can recover some "typical" fantasies, it is because the historical life of the subject is not the prime mover, but rather something antecedent, which is capable of operating as an organizer.
>   Freud saw only one possible explanation of this antecedence, and that was phylogenesis. . . . Thus once again a reality is postulated beneath the elaborations of fantasy, but a reality which, as Freud insists, has an autonomous and structural status with regard to the subject who is totally dependent on it. He pursues this some considerable way, since he admits the possibility of discordance

between the schema and individual experiences, which would lead to psychological conflict.

It is tempting to accept the "reality" which inspires the work of imagination according to its own laws, as a prefiguration of the "symbolic order" defined by Lévi-Strauss and Lacan in the ethnological and psychoanalytic fields respectively. . . . Beneath the pseudo-scientific mask of phylogenesis, or the recourse to "inherited memory-traces," we should have to admit that Freud finds it necessary to postulate an organization made of signifiers anteceding the effect of the event and the signified as a whole.[23]

Laplanche and Pontalis's structural reading of Freud's schemata hypothesis folds back on the concept of the mechanism of deferred action and on the break with the archaeological model this concept brings about. The theories of the formation of unconscious fantasy, presented above, and of *Nachträglichkeit* call into question the idea that the ultimate cause of neurosis is to be sought in an original experience "buried deep beneath," which may be brought to light in psychoanalytic therapy. At the same time, Laplanche and Pontalis's reading of the production of unconscious fantasy introduces a new perspective that may in turn clarify the mechanism of deferred action. This new perspective is the assumption that the reality the analyst is in search of is dispersed in language rather than hidden in the depths of the mind. To Laplanche and Pontalis the fantasy of the primal scene is a story about origins that does not arise from individual experience, but comes into being as individual experience is transcribed in accordance with a preexistant symbolic "schema," or a preexistant narrative, as I prefer to put it.

Apart from the case of the Wolf Man, the case of Emma, presented in part two of *Project for a Scientific Psychology*, remains Freud's most elaborate discussion of *Nachträglichkeit*. I introduce this case story, which shows pronounced similarities with the case of the Wolf Man, because it may illustrate the mechanisms we have discussed above and thereby contribute to the understanding of the Wolf Man's primal scene. *Project for a Scientific Psychology* was written in 1895; the case of Emma and the case of the Wolf Man are thus situated on either side of what is otherwise claimed to be the most important epistemological dividing line in psychoanalysis: Freud's renunciation, in 1897, of the seduction theory and, as a consequence, his "discovery" of infantile sexuality.

This assumption of an epistemological break in Freudian thinking may, however, be queried. First of all, it may be argued that Freud from the very beginning called in question the adequacy of the seduction theory. What is so remarkable about "The Aetiology of Hysteria" (1896) is not Freud's belief in the material truth of the seduction scenes, but the fact that he undermines his own argument by pointing out that *"hysterical symptoms can only arise with the co-operation of memories."* The role of memory in hysteria introduces the problem of temporal spacing, which cannot be solved within the framework of the seduction theory. Seduction theory fails to explain why "the *memory* of infantile sexual experiences produces such an enormous pathogenic effect, while the actual experience itself has none. . . . None of the later scenes, in which the symptoms arise, are the effective ones; and the experiences which *are* effective have at first no result."[24] Secondly, a reading that brings together the cases of Emma and the Wolf Man shows that the discovery of infantile sexuality in no way invalidates the conclusions that Freud, in 1895, must draw in order to explain the effects of what he saw as "pre-sexual sexual" experience—effects that pertain precisely to the phenomenon of temporal spacing.

Like the Wolf Man, Emma was a phobic—she was afraid of entering shops by herself. Freud's analysis brings to light two scenes, a conscious scene that took place when the patient was about thirteen years old and a much earlier scene that is discovered only through analysis. "On two occasions when she was a child of eight she had gone into a small shop to buy some sweets, and the shopkeeper had grabbed at her genitals through her clothes. In spite of the first experience she had gone there a second time; after the second time she stopped away."[25] The later scene, which occurred at about the age of thirteen and which plays a role that is structurally similar to that of the Wolf Man's anxiety dream, is represented as follows: "she went into a shop to buy something, saw the two shop-assistants (one of whom she can remember) laughing together, and ran away in some kind of *affect of fright*" (p. 353; Freud's italics). This scene marked the onset of Emma's phobia. But what caused the phobia? What was the traumatic incident? Laplanche, in his reading of Freud's case in *Life and Death in Psychoanalysis,* stresses the fact that neither of the two scenes, as such, can account for Emma's reaction.

> Neither of the two events in itself is traumatic; neither is a rush of excitation. The first one? It triggers nothing: neither excitation or reaction, nor symbolization or psychical elaboration; we saw why: the child, at the time she is the object of an adult assault, *would not yet possess the ideas necessary to comprehend it.* . . . If the first event is not traumatic, the second is, if possible, even less so. . . . And yet it is that second scene which releases the excitation by awakening the memory of the first one.[26]

In order to explain the outbreak of phobia, one has to take into account the temporal barrier that inscribes the two scenes in *"two different spheres of meaning."*[27] The second scene was no simple repetition or reactivation of the first scene; it was the second scene that enabled Emma to read into the first scene a sexual meaning it did not have, for her, at the time it was experienced. "[I]t is highly noteworthy that it [the sexual release] was not linked to the assault when this was experienced," writes Freud. "Here we have the case of a memory arousing an affect which it did not arouse as an experience, because in the meantime the change [brought about] in puberty had made possible a different understanding of what was remembered" (p. 356). Thus Emma's reaction to the two shop assistants did not merely indicate the return of the repressed childhood event, but a "re-transcription" of the first scene. As Freud writes in a letter to Fliess (December 6, 1896): "I am working on the assumption that . . . the material present in the form of memory-traces being subjected from time to time to a *re-arrangement* in accordance with fresh circumstances—to a *re-transcription*."[28] Actually, up till the second scene, the first scene was a memory trace without any traumatic meaning attached to it; the first scene was not yet repressed. The second scene triggered the significant reworking of the first event as well as its repression. In other words, the scene that seems merely to reactivate the traumatic childhood scene did in fact turn this scene into the trauma. "Now this case is typical of repression in hysteria," writes Freud in his analysis of the case. "We invariably find that a memory is repressed which has only become a trauma by *deferred action*" (p. 356; Freud's italics).

According to Laplanche, puberty is the barrier that separates the two scenes. But Emma's "different understanding" should not merely be seen as an effect of her biological development; Laplanche ignores the importance of the culturally determined stories of gender and sexuality that frame her case. Let us take a closer look at the second shop scene, occurring at the age of thirteen. Why did the two shop assistants laugh? Did their amusement have a sexual undertone? An obscene joke, perhaps, the occasion of which was Emma's presence in the shop? According to Freud, obscene jokes are disguised sexual advances; the woman who is the object of the joke is in fact the person addressed through the joke. Emma's abrupt departure, in that case, made sense: she turned down a sexual proposal. More importantly, she realized that she, as a child of eight, failed to turn down a sexual proposal. Thus in his outline of the case story Freud stresses the importance of the fact that the child, after the assault, had returned to the shop. During the analysis, she "reproached herself for having gone there the second time, as though she had wanted in that way to *provoke* the assault" (p. 354; my italics).

The shop scene at the age of thirteen, then, did not simply bring about a sexualization of the childhood scene. The young girl had not merely acquired "the ideas necessary to comprehend it"; she structured the childhood memory in accordance with a preexistant pattern of interpretation that compelled her to represent herself not as victim of the assault, but as the guilty party. The plot structure she applied to the event was not that of an adult male (subject) assaulting a small girl (object), but that of a female (subject) provoking an outburst of male desire (object). The childhood event triggered the phobia, not only because it retroactively became a sexual event, but because there was no role for Emma in this sexual story except the role as "she who provoked the assault." The childhood event retroactively became a trauma as it was situated within a more comprehensive narrative of male and female sexuality; Emma's trauma was the product of a retranscription, brought about by the application of a subsequently acquired narrative scheme to the reactivated memory of the childhood event.

Structurally, there seems to be no difference between, on the one hand, Emma's belated "plotting" of the first shop scene and, on the other hand, the Wolf Man's belated plotting of his primal scene, in accordance with a particular concept of masculinity and femininity that precipitated his sexual conflict: "He understood now that active was the same as masculine, while passive was the same as feminine" (p. 47). And yet there is one important difference: In the case of Emma, the significant interaction was between two scenes separated by the onset of puberty. In the case of the Wolf Man, it was the anxiety dream at the age of four that marked the "re-transcription" of the scene originally experienced at the age of one and a half years. The notion of deferred action has been retained—but the discovery of infantile sexuality seems to have relegated this mechanism to the years of early childhood. Maybe this is not the case, after all. We should not forget that the Wolf Man's first scene is, strictly speaking, neither a memory that was subsequently interpreted nor an infantile fantasy that the patient "has created . . . for himself." The primal scene, around which the entire analysis revolves and which controls the interpretation of every piece of material brought forth during the treatment, remains an analytical construction. The significant interaction may thus not be between two events from the patient's childhood, but between the scene constructed in the analysis and the memories and fantasies the patient has produced.

Having outlined the Wolf Man's primal scene, Freud goes on to say that the patient, when he "entered more deeply into the situation of the primal scene," responded by bringing to light "the following pieces of self-observation. He assumed to begin with, he said, that the event of which he was a witness was an act of violence, but the expression of enjoyment which he saw on his mother's face did not fit with this; he was obliged to recognize that the experience was one of gratification" (p. 45). Thus the Wolf Man, at the age of twenty-five, responded to the primal scene—which had emerged as a construction in the analytical dialogue and which he could not be brought to remember—by completing Freud's account of this scene. Moreover, he brought to light an observation of which he was not capable at the time of the anxiety dream, let alone at the time when the primal scene was supposed to take place. Freud, in a footnote, writes:

> We must not forget the actual situation which lies behind the abbreviated description given in the text: the patient under analysis, at an age of over twenty-five years, was putting the impressions and impulses of his fourth year into words which he would never have found at that time. If we fail to notice this, it may easily seem comic and incredible that a child of four should be capable of such technical judgements and learned notions. This is simply another instance of *deferred action*. At the age of one and a half the child receives an impression to which he is unable to react adequately; he is only able to understand it and to be moved by it when the impression is revived in him at the age of four; and only twenty years later, during the analysis, is he able to grasp with his conscious mental processes what was then going on in him. The patient justifiably disregards the three periods of time, and puts his present ego into the situation which is so long past. And in this we follow him, since with correct self-observation and interpretation the effect must be the same as though the distance between the second and third periods of time could be neglected. Moreover, we have no other means of describing the events of the second period. (p. 45, note 1; Freud's italics)

What is suggested, then, is that the analytical situation itself is submitted to the logic of *Nachträglichkeit*. The patient's self-observation in analysis is said to be nothing but "another instance of *deferred action*"; it was a belated interpretation applied, across a temporal gap of almost twenty years, to the infantile (nonrecollected) scene, and which, as the temporal distance is disregarded, retroactively became one with the scene itself. The psychical effects of the primal scene appear to be bound up with the patient's neglect of temporal distance, and yet temporal spacing—the "periods" to which Freud is referring—seems to be required for the emergence of the primal scene as original trauma. Far from being a timeless, unchanging content, the repressed material appears to be submitted to a series of revisionary, supplementary actions. In fact, the meaning of the primal scene is shown to depend on the position of this scene in a complex—and open—network of relations between different elements. The past that is the object of the psychoanalytic quest is not simply there, it is not simply an unchanging object waiting to be brought to light through the "work of the spades." The past of which the analysis is in search comes into being only after the event; it has no final meaning but is, in principle, the object of an infinite series of retroactive rereadings.

Freud suggests that the Wolf Man's "self-observation" represents a deferred, adult understanding of his already deferred understanding, at the age of four years, of the impressions he received but failed to understand at the age of one and a half. But is it necessarily so? Again, we should not forget that the patient in analysis was not filling in gaps in memory; he was elaborating on the analytical construction he had been offered. The Wolf Man's self-observation was an instance of indirect confirmation of the hypothetical construction; it was an attempt to "complete and extend the construction."[29] And a very significant and interesting extension, indeed.

In fact, the Wolf Man introduced a new, complementary, visual representation of the coitus scene; he introduced a new perspective, as it were. The primal scene has previously been described as follows: "he witnessed a coitus *a tergo,* three times repeated; he was able to see his mother's genitals as well as his father's organ" (p. 37). The new version of the scene says that he saw "the expression of enjoyment . . . on his mother's face." Thus the two statements seem to exclude each other: if the child observed the intercourse from a position that allowed him to see his parents' genitals, would he then, simultaneously, be able to study the expression on his mother's face? Freud is aware of this apparent contradiction and seeks to explain it by suggesting that the parents' position during the intercourse was altered. But "this hypothesis . . . was not confirmed with certainty, and moreover does not seem to me indispensable" (p. 45, note 1). An alternative explanation would be that the Wolf Man's observation was an observation of a more recent date that was applied retroactively to the primal scene. That is to say, the primal scene was interpreted through a filter of subsequent sexual experiences. Much more important, however, is the fact that the Wolf Man's observation introduced an element that supported that part of Freud's interpretation of the infantile conflict for which the first version of the primal scene did not account.

The first version deals with mutilation, the "castrated" mother (genitals); the second version is about sexual gratification (facial expression). From a "realistic" point of view, the two observations seem to be mutually exclusive. The Wolf Man's completion of the primal scene, then, does not prove its authenticity; in fact his observation seems to impede the attempt to determine what the child "actually" saw. Taken together, however, the two versions form a dual perspective, which becomes the figure of "the space of sexual undecidability"[30] and which dramatizes the conflict, at the center of the infantile neurosis, that Freud's interpretation has postulated. We may, he writes, represent the Wolf Man as saying to himself: "'*If you want to be sexually satisfied by Father,*'" (which is attractive, identification with the expression of enjoyment on his mother's face), "'*you must allow yourself to be castrated like Mother; but I won't have that.*' In short, a clear protest on the part of his masculinity" (p. 47; my italics). Through his observation, the Wolf Man had supplied what was missing from the construction the analyst had offered him, and thereby sealed his acceptance of Freud's interpretation of the infantile neurosis.

From the History of an Infantile Neurosis, then, invites us to conceive of a certain structural similarity between fantasizing, constructing, and verifying—or, more precisely, between the creation of primal fantasies, of primal scenes of origin, the analyst's construction of the lost origin, and, finally, the analysand's "indirect . . . confirmation" of this construction.[31] Each is poised between, on the one hand, a material composed of experiences, observations, impulses, and memories and, on the other hand, an intervening interpretive schema, "concerned with the business of 'placing' the impressions derived from actual experiences." As the children "in their phantasies are . . . filling in the gaps in individual truth" in conformity with antecedent schemata, so does the analyst construct "by means of supplementing and combining."[32] And just as the analyst restores "what is missing, taking the best models . . . from other analyses,"[33] so does the analysand complete this construction by filling in the gaps in accordance with the interpretive "schema" of psychoanalytic theory.

The impossibility of definitively establishing what the child saw foregrounds the question of "the significance of the infantile factor" (p. 54) and the "importance of early infantile impressions" (p. 49) that is the topic of Freud's *Auseinandersetzung* with Jung and Adler. Jung and Adler had maintained that the causes of neuroses must be sought in the conflicts of later life. According to this, the Wolf Man's primal scene should be seen as an instance of regressive or retrospective fantasizing, that is, as a fantasy from the patient's mature years that had been projected back into early childhood. But, claims Freud, behind this

attempt to explain away the role of infantile experience lurks a far
more serious allegation against the analyst: "What is argued now is
evidently that they [the childhood scenes] are phantasies, not of the
patient but of the analyst himself, who forces them upon the person
under analysis on account of some complexes of his own" (p. 52).
Freud's reply to his opponents is unusually sharp.

First of all, he makes it absolutely clear that either one accepts the
idea of the primal scene, or the analysis "is all a piece of nonsense from
start to finish" (p. 56). In the context of a case story that refuses to make
a definite choice between fantasy and real event and that systematically
undermines linear causality, this rejection of the theory of retrospective fantasizing may seem surprising. Freud's remark should, I think,
be taken as a statement on the necessity of assuming, as a theoretical
hypothesis, the existence of an original, infantile scene. Also, it should
be noted that he later adopts a much less exclusive position on the issue
of retrospective fantasy. In one of the numerous footnotes (which so
often reintroduce the doubt the text itself appears to have removed)
he writes:

> I admit that this [the question of retrospective fantasizing] is the
> most delicate question in the whole domain of psycho-analysis. I
> did not require the contributions of Adler or Jung to induce me to
> consider the matter with a critical eye, and to bear in mind the
> possibility that what analysis puts forward as being forgotten expe-
> riences of childhood (and of an improbably early childhood) may
> on the contrary be based upon phantasies created on occasions
> occurring late in life. . . . On the contrary, no doubt has troubled
> me more; no other uncertainty has been more decisive in hold-
> ing me back from publishing my conclusions. I was the first . . .
> to recognize both the part played by phantasies in symptom-
> formation and also the "retrospective phantasying" of late impres-
> sions into childhood and their sexualization after the event. (p.
> 103, note 1)

Secondly, Freud strongly repudiates the allegation of having
forced the primal scene on the patient:

> An analyst, indeed, who hears this reproach, will comfort himself
> by recalling how gradually the construction of this phantasy which
> he is supposed to have originated came about, and, when all is said
> and done, how independently of the physician's incentive many
> points in its development proceeded; how, after a certain phase of
> the treatment, everything seemed to converge upon it, and how

later, in the synthesis, the most various and remarkable results radiated out from it; how not only the large problems but the smallest peculiarities in the history of the case were cleared up by this single assumption. And he will disclaim the possession of the amount of ingenuity necessary for the concoction of an occurrence which can fulfil all these demands. (p. 52)

But while Freud, on the one hand, denies the charge of having invented the primal scene, he, on the other hand, does not claim that this scene belongs exclusively to the patient. From the very beginning he has made it clear that the analytic construction emerges from the analytical dialogue, and that this dialogue is based on an unspoken contract between analyst and analysand that can be broken by either party. The analysand can keep silent and thus refuse to collaborate. In fact the Wolf Man "remained for a long time unassailably entrenched behind an attitude of obliging apathy. He listened, understood, and remained unapproachable" (p. 11). The first years of the treatment produced scarcely any results. "I was obliged to wait until his attachment to myself had become strong enough to counter-balance this shrinking" (p. 11). At that point the analyst threatened to stop the treatment, and not until then did the Wolf Man produce the material that made possible the interpretation of the anxiety dream.

The analytical construction is situated within this space of transference and countertransference. It sustains and is sustained by the relationship between analyst and analysand; it renews the contract that makes possible the continuation of the treatment, which otherwise would have been broken off prematurely; and it provides the analyst and the analysand with a shared frame of reference that enables the dialogue to go on. This, then, is the context in which we should read the Wolf Man's primal scene: it is an analytical construction that belongs neither to the analyst (as Jung and Adler would have it) nor to the analysand, but to both. As the Wolf Man's "self-observation" indicates, this analytic construction finally assumes the status of something that "*must* be believed."[34] The primal scene is appropriated by the patient and operates in the present as though it were a recaptured memory of the event that precipitated his infantile neurosis.

In his dispute with Jung and Adler, Freud points out that the hypothesis of the primal scene during the analytical treatment was confirmed by a series of dreams, all of which led back to this scene as they reproduced "every portion of its content in an inexhaustible variety of new shapes" (p. 51). Unfortunately, *From the History of an Infantile Neurosis* does not provide us with any insight into these subsequent dreams, but apparently Freud is alluding to dreams dreamt in response to his interpretation of the wolf dream, because he goes on to say that he is aware of the fact that "dreams can be guided" (p. 52) or influenced by the analyst. In "Remarks on the Theory and Practice of Dream-Interpretation" we find a more elaborate discussion of this issue. Of course it is possible to exert an influence on the latent dream thoughts, writes Freud; as is well known, parts of these latent dream thoughts are conscious or preconscious thoughts or bits and pieces of fresh impressions. But what about those dream thoughts that pertain to the dreamer's childhood: can this part of the dream also be guided? Is it, in other words, possible for the analyst to exert an influence on the dreams that seem to confirm analytical constructions of the patient's past? Freud writes:

> If a dream brings up situations that can be interpreted as referring to scenes from the dreamer's past, it seems especially important to ask whether the physician's influence can also play a part in such contents of the dream as these. And the question is most urgent of all in the case of what are called "corroborative" dreams, dreams which, as it were, "tag along behind" the analysis. With some patients these are the only dreams that one obtains. Such patients reproduce the forgotten experiences of their childhood only after one has constructed them from their symptoms, associations and other signs and has propounded these constructions to them. Then follow the corroborative dreams, concerning which, however, the doubt arises whether they may not be entirely without evidential value, since they may have been imagined in compliance with the physician's words instead of having been brought to light from the dreamer's unconscious. This ambiguous position cannot be escaped in the analysis, since with these patients unless one interprets, constructs and propounds, one never obtains access to what is repressed in them.[35]

In fact, there is only one thing the analyst cannot influence, namely, the dream work itself.[36] There is no escape, then, from ambiguity. The attempt to anchor the construction in a reality properly outside the analytical situation reveals that, in analysis, there is no such reality that does not involve the relationship between analyst and analysand. As evidence of the factual existence of the primal scene, the "corroborative" dreams are indeed useless. However, these dreams dreamt during analysis produce an effect that is of utmost importance to the treatment. "It is this recurrence in dreams that I regard as the explanation of the fact that the patients themselves gradually acquire a profound conviction of the reality of these primal scenes, a conviction which is in no respect inferior to one based on recollection" (p. 51). The Wolf Man's "corroborative" dreams and his completion of the primal scene are indications of the fact that he had appropriated the construction.

Freud's significant rewording of this proposition in the paragraph cited above points to a new understanding of the dynamics of the analytic construction: the patient's "profound conviction" of the "reality" of the constructed scene is an effect of the recurrence of this scene in dreams. In order to carry conviction, the primal scene—which was originally presented to the patient from without—must return from within. The primal scene that by deferred action has been assimilated into the past itself recurs in the form of dreaming, which Freud has described as "another kind of remembering" (p. 51).

As will be remembered, the discussion in the fifth chapter of *From the History of an Infantile Neurosis,* of the epistemological status of the primal scene closes with a *non liquet.* In chapter 8 Freud picks up the thread of this discussion, as he introduces a new scene. Toward the end of the treatment, the Wolf Man brought to light a memory dating from his early childhood (before the wolf dream); his nurserymaid, Grusha, "was kneeling on the floor, and beside her a pail and a short broom made of a bundle of twigs; he was also there, and she was teasing him or scolding him" (p. 91). The recollection was "incomplete," but the "missing elements could easily be supplied from other directions " (p. 91). The remembered scene was nothing but an early—in fact the first—reaction to the primal scene, claims Freud, and he goes on to (re)construct the incident as follows: "When he saw the girl scrubbing the floor he had micturated in the room and she had rejoined, no doubt jokingly, with a threat of castration" (p. 92). The child

> was faced once again with the posture which his mother had assumed in the copulation scene. She [Grusha] became his mother to him; he was seized with sexual excitement owing to the activation of this picture; and, like his father (whose action he can only have regarded at the time as micturition), he behaved in a masculine way towards her. His micturition on the floor was in reality an attempt at a seduction, and the girl replied to it with a threat of castration, just as though she had understood what he meant. (pp. 92–93)

This reconstruction of the Grusha scene has given rise to several critical commentaries. Thus Jacobsen and Steele, as well as Spence, discuss the scene at length, arguing that Freud's interpretation is an

instance of unwitting distortion in analysis. The Grusha scene is a
reconstruction, writes Spence, which in the course of Freud's interpretation "quickly became absorbed into the memory itself; what began as an hypothesis about the past became part of the past."[37] The
scene is only comprehensible as a construction of a type that forges a
link with the primal scene, in itself not a real event but a hypothesis
that, in the words of Jacobsen and Steele, "is necessitated only by other
interpretations and constructions in the case which have created a
causal web into which the primal scene must be inserted."[38] It is the
primal scene that determines the analyst's attempt to supply what is
missing from the analysand's recollection. The Grusha scene is thus a
construction within a construction, a referential hypothesis within a
referential hypothesis. And yet, as Spence points out, this construction
is given the status of an authentic memory. Thus Freud goes on to talk
about "*the fact* that the boy micturated" (p. 96; my italics). But are we to
conclude that Freud's interpretation distorts the case? A more produc-
tive approach would be to regard the status of the Grusha scene as a
problem analogous with the problem of the status of the primal scene.

I have previously cited different views on Freud's refusal to make a
definite choice between his two explanations of the primal scene as
either a real event subsequently invested with traumatic meaning or as
an unconscious fantasy. On the one hand, the impossibility of making a
final choice is claimed to be of no importance, since both versions "give
us very similar narratives" (Culler). On the other hand, the coexistence
in Freud's text of two explanations is said to engender "a structure of
indeterminacy" (Brooks). Indeed, as regards the course of the treatment itself, it makes little difference whether the primal scene is given
the status of an infantile fantasy or of a real event. In the fictive space of
analysis—the space of "as though"—fantasies are just as real as real
events. "The analysis would have run precisely the same course as one
which had a *naïf* faith in the truth of the phantasies," writes Freud.
"The difference would only come at the end of the analysis, after the
phantasies had been laid bare" (p. 50).

As regards the question of psychoanalytic truth and of reading in
psychoanalysis, however, the ambiguity of his answer articulates a crisis
of interpretation; the relationship between the events of the past and
the analytical narration of the past is recognized to be neither unproblematic nor unequivocal. Freud's position as regards the Grusha scene
should be considered in the context of his oscillation between these two
levels of discourse, the account of the course of the treatment and his
discussion (with Jung and Adler) of psychoanalytic epistemology. The
"*naïf* faith" in the reality of the Grusha scene he seems to adopt reflects,
I think, this split between therapy and theorizing.

What is so remarkable about *From the History of an Infantile Neurosis* is the fact that Freud allows his doubts to interfere with and even, at times, to undermine his argument; the psychoanalyst gives up the advantage of "the scientific monologue, the unchallenged voice of truth."[39] On the one hand, he would of course prefer to be able to present the primal scene as a real event from the patient's early childhood. On the other hand, he deconstructs the dichotomy of real event and fantasy and allows for the coexistence of different and mutually exclusive readings. In fact, he who cannot endure the undecidability, who refuses to see the constructed scenes as anything but real events, is the *patient* himself. Having completed his interpretation of the Grusha scene, Freud, "out of critical interest," as he puts it, turns to his patient with alternative readings of the Grusha scene and the primal scene. The Grusha scene, it is suggested, meant nothing in itself; it "had been emphasized *ex post facto* by a regression from the circumstances of his object-choice" (p. 95), and as regards the primal scene, it "was a phantasy of his later years" (p. 95). The patient, Freud goes on to say, "looked at me uncomprehendingly and a little contemptuously when I put this view before him, and he never reacted to it again" (p. 95). Thus with the assimilation of the Grusha scene, "the treatment had every appearance of having being solved. From that time forward there were no more resistances; all that remained to be done was to collect and to co-ordinate" (pp. 94–95). It is interesting to note, however, that the patient's acceptance of the constructions does not mean the end to Freud's discussion of the epistemological status of these scenes. The Wolf Man's acceptance, which marks the completion of the treatment, does not bring to a conclusion the inquiry to which his case has given rise.

One story line of *From the History of an Infantile Neurosis* is the history of the treatment; another is the discussion of the case itself. At this level of discourse we find Freud playing *fort da* with his hypotheses: one reading is supplanted by another, but only in order to resurface. It is not surprising, then, that the chapter that seems to close the case, "Fresh Material from the Primal Period—Solution," is followed by a final chapter, "Recapitulations and Problems," which, as it introduces the schema hypothesis that I have discussed above, once again unsettles the case that appeared to have been solved. Nor is it surprising that the readings the Wolf Man so firmly had rejected (and which were never again alluded to in the treatment) reappear in the context of the meta-analytical reflections.

In one of the paragraphs added in 1918, Freud returns to the Grusha scene. There seems little doubt that this scene was a real event, he maintains; but was it originally a sexual scene? Was the act of micturition (which he continues to represent as an established fact) a sign of sexual excitement on the part of the boy?

> If so, the excitement would be evidence of the influence of an earlier impression, which might equally have been the actual occurrence of the primal scene or an observation made upon animals before the age of two and a half. Or are we to conclude that the situation as regards Grusha was entirely innocent, that the child's emptying his bladder was purely accidental, and that it was not until later that the whole scene became sexualized in his memory, after he had come to recognize the importance of similar situations? (p. 96)

Freud's doubt gets the last word. "On these issues I can venture upon no decision," he says (p. 96).

Thus an interminable or open-ended story, which may be called the story of Freud's doubts, is grafted upon the story that demands closure, namely the therapeutical story, and this twofold structure suggests that we should regard the closure of the treatment as provisional or pragmatic rather than final. Closure and coherency appear to be essential to the patient, according to whom there is only one valid story: the history of the infantile neurosis, which has been pieced together laboriously in the course of the analysis and which implies the truth of the scenes that cannot be remembered. To the Wolf Man, the primal scene has assumed the effects of the real; it has assumed the status of a recaptured memory. "The primal scene has come into being as the cooperative construct of the Wolf-Man and his analyst," writes Kartiganer, but, at this point, "no one, not even Freud, can take it away."[40]

The end of the treatment, the closure of the story of the Wolf Man, does not imply that a final truth has been obtained. As Freud's return to the case in "Analysis Terminable and Interminable" suggests, new plots may always be created which, quite in accordance with the logic of deferred action, may alter the meaning of the forgotten past as well as its present effects. The implication of all this is an understanding of the analytical process that calls into question the story of psychoanalysis as an archaeology of the soul. The case of the Wolf Man tells the story of that which is left unaccounted for in the archaeological version of reading in psychoanalysis; it brings to the center that which this version has marginalized. In so doing, *From the History of an Infantile Neurosis* installs a new figure: the archaeological metaphor is replaced by the metaphor of the *Zwischenreich*—or, in Brooks's translation, the "in-between." The primal scene "lies in-between."[41] It is situated between the events of the past and the significant "re-transcription" of these events. It belongs within the differential space of *Nachträglichkeit*, which encompasses the dialogical space of analysis.

Part Three
Psychoanalysis and
Literature

Chapter 4

Gradiva: Textual Archaeology and the Ghost of Fiction

Let me once again turn to *Delusions and Dreams in Jensen's* Gradiva. I have previously discussed this work in light of the psychoanalytic process, arguing that Freud construes Jensen's novel as the emblematic story of psychoanalysis as archaeology of the soul. The present chapter considers his reading of *Gradiva* as a piece of psychoanalytic literary criticism and a contribution to psychoanalytic literary theory. True, questions of psychoanalysis and literature play a secondary role in Freud's argument. Jensen's novel is first of all called upon to support the insights of the dream theory, and in his postscript to the second edition of *Delusions and Dreams in Jensen's* Gradiva, Freud makes a point of distinguishing the purpose of his reading of *Gradiva* from the purpose of what may be called a psychoanalytic literary interpretation proper. In the years that have passed since the publication of *Delusions and Dreams in Jensen's* Gradiva, psychoanalysis "has summoned up the courage to approach the creations of imaginative writers with yet another purpose in view." The psychoanalyst no longer merely seeks in works of fiction for "confirmations" of his "findings"; he "also demands to know the material of impressions and memories from which the author has built the work, and the methods and processes by which he has converted this material into a work of art."[1] It appears, however, that this purpose is built into a reading that merely seeks confirmation of psychoanalytic theory. For in order to show that the author of *Gradiva* agrees with psychoanalysis on the issue of dreams having a meaning, Freud must bring to light the hidden meaning of his work; in order to explain *Gradiva*'s remarkable psychoanalytic insights, he must inquire into the psychic source of the author's inspiration. Indeed, in order to represent *Gradiva* as a faithful account of a psychoanalytic process, he must examine the text with the methods it supposedly thematizes.

In the following, I shall discuss the strategies of interpretation Freud employs in order to uncover the "psychoanalytic knowledge" of Jensen's "Fantasy," as well as the conception of the relationship between psychoanalysis and literature that underlies his approach. Reading is my main issue: not the psychoanalyst's reading of his patient, but his reading of a work of fiction. However, my intention is to show that Freud's approach to *Gradiva* as a literary text is closely associated with the archaeological model of the psychoanalytic process he recognizes in Jensen's story: in order to read the novel as a "psychiatric study" of repression, symptom formation, and cure, Freud, as reader of *Gradiva*, must assume the place of Zoe-the-analyst; in order to represent Jensen's "Pompeian Fantasy" as a faithful account of an archaeological psychoanalytic process, he must conceive of his own interpretation of the novel as what may be called an "archaeology of the text." Freud's interpretation of *Gradiva* (or rather of Zoe's analysis of Norbert) as the emblematic story of the psychoanalytic therapeutic process, then, is by the same token his construction of the narrative as allegory of its own (psychoanalytic) reading.

In Zoe's clever "excavation" of Norbert Hanold's "inner Pompeii," Freud finds a model of the psychoanalyst's exposure of the repressed past, as well as of his exposure of the hidden meaning of the fictional text. But *Delusions and Dreams in Jensen's* Gradiva (considered as a piece of practical criticism) fails to conform to this model. Through a detailed analysis of Freud's argument, Sarah Kofman has disclosed a discrepancy between, on the one hand, the emblematic story of psychoanalytic interpretation he recognizes in *Gradiva* and, on the other hand, his own interpretation of Jensen's text. That is, she identifies a discrepancy between what Freud says (about psychoanalytic interpretation) and what he does (as reader of Jensen's narrative). The analyst desires interpretive mastery of the text, but, says Kofman, "Le psychanalyste ne détient ni la clef de l'oeuvre ni la vérité: Il n'est pas Zoé."[2] Freud does not possess Zoe's hermeneutical authority; he does not have privileged access to the deepest levels of meaning of the text. But is Zoe, in the story of reading Freud constructs, in fact in possession of the final truth? Does she have privileged access to the past? In the last part of this chapter, I shall show how Freud, in an attempt to claim final hermeneutical power over the text, arrives at an interpretation of Zoe/Gradiva that inadvertently undermines Zoe's authority and, indeed, is on the verge of overthrowing his own reading of the narrative. One may argue, therefore, that this first full-length psychoanalytic interpretation of a fictional text fails on its own premises. But one should add that, from the perspective of literary criticism, this reading of *Gradiva* succeeds precisely because it fails to master the text. Freud very accurately points out the blind spot of his own interpretation. From this blind spot emerges the "ghost of fiction," that is, the problem of fictionality the psychoanalytic approach has ignored.

The story of reading Freud finds in Wilhelm Jensen's *Gradiva* is not only an account of forgetting and remembering that links up this twofold process with the fate of Pompeii. It is, by the same token, the story of a work of art, enveloped in a powerful poetical fantasy, which is traced back to its living original. Norbert Hanold's dream of Gradiva in Pompeii may once again serve as our point of departure. We have seen how Freud reads this dream as an allegory of repression, or more precisely as an allegory of the analogy between the mental process of repression and "burial of the sort to which Pompeii fell a victim and from which it could emerge once more through the work of the spades."[3] But repression, in the case of Norbert, took the form of the transformation of Zoe into the ancient work of art. "Hanold had in fact transferred his interest from the living girl to the sculpture: the girl he loved had been transformed for him into a marble relief" (p. 60). In the dream Norbert saw Gradiva as a dying inhabitant of the dying town. Her "face became paler as if it were changing to white marble." Her countenance, stifled, "was like that of a beautiful statue." However, as Freud points out, the dream did in fact represent the Gradiva relief as a woman of flesh and blood; and, moreover, it represented her as Norbert's "contemporary." The dreamer, reasons the psychoanalyst, "sought to change the sculpture back into the living girl" (p. 60). This, then, is the story line I pursue in the following: the metamorphosis of the living woman into the marble woman, and the emergence, through the work of interpretation, of the real woman from the work of art.

As Freud's paraphrase makes clear, the love of art, in this novel, is a perversion as well as a delusion. For "was not our hero's infatuation for his Gradiva sculpture a complete instance of being in love, though of being in love with something past and lifeless?" (p. 22). Immersing himself so deeply in the study of classical art that he has turned away from "life and its pleasures" (p. 14), Norbert has developed an unnatural passion for dead works of art. Classical art has become superior to present reality, or rather it has become life itself. "Marble and bronze alone were truly alive for him," writes Freud, "they alone expressed the purpose and value of human life" (p. 14). Presented with the choice between women of flesh and blood and sculpted women, the young archaeologist chooses the work of art. On his journey to Italy, he finds himself making comparisons, and in every way real women fall short of "the sublime beauty of the old works of art."[4] To Norbert, contemporary women are but poor imitations of ancient women made of marble and bronze, and he shows a profound contempt for the honeymooning Gretchens and Augustuses crowding the hotels of Rome and Naples, to whom real bodies "are much more pleasing than Apollo Belvedere" and "much more beautiful than the Capitoline Venus."[5]

But, as we know, Norbert himself ends up as a honeymooner. Toward the end of the novel, he suggests that he and Zoe should spend their honeymoon in Italy. The young archaeologist has thus identified with the "Augustuses" whom he once despised. The cure of his delusion coincides with the fact that a real female body has become more attractive to him than the sublime beauty of the relief; his love for Gradiva is displaced to Zoe. Norbert's delusion, says Freud, "had now been conquered by a beautiful reality" (p. 39). And asking Zoe to go ahead of him so that he can admire her graceful gait—the characteristic gait that once made the Gradiva relief so irresistible to him—Norbert seals his return to reality: Gradiva has been reduced to a harmless aesthetical supplement.

Commenting on the "great transformation" (p. 39) that has taken place in the young archaeologist, Freud remarks that the Gradiva relief has been replaced by the woman of whom "it could only have been a distorted and inadequate copy" (p. 37). Thus Zoe was the sculpted image's original. In transferring his interest from the lifeless relief to the living woman, Norbert has rediscovered his first love; the real meaning of his unnatural passion was his unrecognized love for the girl next door. The world of classical art, then, was the instrument for forgetting as well as for the displaced return of that which has been forgotten: the return of Zoe in the guise of the ancient relief.

> If Norbert Hanold were someone in real life who had in this way banished love and his childhood friendship with the help of archaeology, it would have been logical and according to rule that what revived in him the forgotten memory of the girl he had loved in his childhood should be precisely an antique sculpture. It would have been his well-deserved fate to fall in love with the marble portrait of Gradiva, behind which, owing to an unexplained similarity, the living Zoe whom he had neglected made her influence felt. (pp. 36–37)

The state of permanently turning away from women produces, says Freud, a disposition to the formation of a delusion. Norbert's preference for women of marble and bronze to women of flesh and blood is thus not to be regarded as a "trivial peculiarity"; on the contrary, it was the "basic precondition" for the archaeologist's belief that the woman he encountered in Pompeii was the model of the relief and had returned from the land of the dead. Norbert's perverted attachment to a lifeless relief, the fantasies that he weaved around Gradiva, and the delusion into which these fantasies were magnified were successive stages of the same process; imagination gradually gained the upper hand. The archaeologist became himself a "creator," constructing a powerful fiction he could not separate from real life. Norbert Hanold's "kingdom is not of this world," writes Freud; nature had provided him with "an extremely lively imagination, which could show itself not only in his dreams but often in his waking life as well. This division between imagination and intellect destined him to become an artist or a neurotic" (p. 14). Perversion, fantasy, and delusion were different aspects of the same mental disposition; they derived their power from the same source, and they obeyed the same laws. In each case we find a "double set of determinants":

> Thus in the very first products of Hanold's delusional phantasies and actions we already find a double set of determinants, a derivation from two different sources. One of these is the one that was manifest to Hanold himself, the other is the one which is revealed to us when we examine his mental processes. One of them, looked at from Hanold's point of view, was conscious to him, the other was completely unconscious to him. One of them was derived wholly from the circle of ideas of the science of archaeology, the other arose from the repressed childhood memories that had become active in him and from the emotional instincts attached to them. One might be described as lying on the surface and covering the other, which was, as it were, concealed behind it. (pp. 51–52)

This, too, applies to Norbert's three dreams. As Freud points out, the dream of Gradiva in Pompeii, which seemed merely a figment of the archaeologist's imagination, did in fact give some valuable information that "tallied with the real state of things" (p. 58).

> The sense is merely disguised in a particular way so that it is not immediately recognizable. Hanold learned in the dream that the girl he was looking for was living in a town and contemporaneously with him. Now this was true of Zoe Bertgang; only in the dream the town was not the German university town but Pompeii, and the time was not the present but the year 79 A.D. It is, as it were, a distortion by displacement: what we have is not Gradiva in the present but the dreamer transported into the past. Neverthe-

less, in this manner, the essential and new fact is stated: *he is in the same place and time as the girl he is looking for.* (p. 58; Freud's italics)

Interpreting a dream, Freud goes on to say,

> consists in translating the manifest content of the dream into the latent dream-thoughts, in undoing the distortion which the dream-thoughts have had to submit to from the censorship of the resistance. If we apply these notions to the dream we are concerned with, we shall find that its latent dream-thoughts can only have been: "the girl you are looking for with the graceful gait is really living in this town with you." (p. 59)

Had Norbert been able to decipher this dream, the story would have come to an end here. But due to the force of repression, he is deceived over its "true meaning and content" (p. 58). The young archaeologist must await the arrival of a reader who can accomplish that which he could not do on his own, a reader who can return to him the message the dream work had disguised and distorted.

Juxtaposing the dreams and fantasies Freud has interpreted for us and Zoe's final "speech of castigation," the "frank, detailed, and instructive" (p. 37) speech that clears up everything, we must draw the conclusion that Norbert and Zoe share the same insight. They express this insight differently, however; the two speak different languages, as it were. In the case of Norbert, an undistorted but objectionable content has been rendered in an enigmatic but unobjectionable figurative language. "It is all there in the dream," writes Freud in his analysis of Norbert's third dream. The information the young archaeologist is in search of "is fully announced in the dream, but so cleverly concealed that it is bound to be overlooked. It is hidden behind a play upon words, an ambiguity" (p. 81). Norbert is obliged to make use of an indirect mode of expression that Freud, having already stated his admiration for the "charm" (p. 14) of the archaeologist's language, prefers to characterize as "an ingenious and poetical representation of the real event" (p. 60).

As a contrast, Zoe's final speech is said to be clear and transparent. "Fräulein Zoe, the embodiment of cleverness and clarity, makes her own mind quite transparent to us" (p. 33). But the plainness and clarity of Zoe's final speech does not prevent her from making use of ambiguities. "Anyone who reads *Gradiva* must be struck by the frequency with which the author puts ambiguous remarks into the mouths of his two principal characters" (p. 84). Her treatment consists of two distinct parts or phases. It is only toward the end of the story that she reveals her true identity. During the first part of her treatment, Zoe appears to accept the role of Gradiva; her language echoes the language of Norbert's delusion. But, as it soon becomes clear to the reader, she has entered her childhood sweetheart's fantasy in order to bring to light the meaning concealed behind his "poetical" statements.

Thus Zoe's use of ambiguities is quite distinct from that of her patient: "In Hanold's case these remarks are intended by him unambiguously and it is only the heroine . . . who is struck by their second meaning" (p. 84). In the case of Norbert, the two meanings are separated by a barrier the speaker is unable to cross. Norbert can only move on the figurative level of language; but, as he cannot grasp their true meaning, he is confined to a quite literal reading of his own poetical figures. His disturbance, one might say, consists in his mistaking the figurative for the literal. The ambiguity of Zoe's speech is, on the other hand, "intentional" (p. 84); from her perspective, ambiguity is an attempt at cure. Zoe adopts the symbolism of Norbert's delusion in order to turn it against itself. She enters his poetical language only in order to disclose to him the truth it hides.

Freud, as it will be remembered, asserts that the story of repression and cure he has extracted from *Gradiva* "might have been designed to emphasize certain fundamental theories of medical psychology" (p. 43). He might have added that Jensen's treatment of the theme of art, fantasy, and reality, as well as his representation of the act of deciphering, might have been designed to emphasize certain fundamental aspects of psychoanalytic literary criticism and theory.

Freud begins his reading of *Gradiva* by calling attention to the problematic nature of his undertaking: Can fictional dreams be interpreted as real dreams? Can psychoanalysis measure its understanding of the workings of the mind on a text described as "genuine poetic material" (p. 10)? His discussion of these issues constitutes a meta-analytical stratum of his interpretation of *Gradiva.* What is at stake here is the question of how fictional constructions are related to the (psychic) reality that is the domain of psychoanalysis. This question, however, is itself part of a more comprehensive problem, namely the problem of defining the relationship between literature and psychoanalysis, between poetical insight and psychoanalytic theory.

As Jean-Louis Baudry has pointed out, Freud's analytical enterprise is caught in a double bind.[6] Having summarized Jensen's narrative, Freud declares that he would not object "if *Gradiva* were described not as a phantasy but as a psychiatric study" (p. 41). Psychoanalysis and literature both explore the same object, the depths of the human soul. Literature conveys a psychological insight more profound than that of so-called science. In their knowledge of the mind the poets "are far in advance of us everyday people, for they draw upon sources which we have not yet opened up for science" (p. 8). But, having praised the "evidence" (p. 8) given by creative writers, Freud goes on to say that a study of *Gradiva* may teach us nothing new about dreams; instead, we may "gain some small insight into the nature of creative writing" (p. 9). And, toward the end of his essay, he points out that he has examined the narrative with "the methods of medical psychoanalysis" (p. 92); Jensen's novel has occupied the place of the analysand in psychoanalytic therapy. Is *Gradiva* then, in Freud's argument, supreme authority? Or is it rather that his approach (as Felman has it) implies the submission of the literary text to the supreme authority of psychoanalysis? Is the literary text the place where knowledge, knowledge of the mind, resides? Or is literature rather the potential object of a psychoanalytic knowledge? *Delusions and Dreams in Jensen's* Gradiva, writes Baudry, will not venture to make a final choice between these alternatives.

And yet it seems to me that Freud seeks to resolve this double bind through his interpretative summary of *Gradiva* as a story of a work of art, concealing and distorting but nevertheless betraying the truth the protagonist had repressed. According to Freud, the author of *Gradiva* does indeed possess remarkable knowledge that confirms psychoanalytic theory. But, as I shall argue, this insight is recognized to be structurally analogous with the truth contained in the Gradiva relief and in Norbert's poetical delusions: it is "hidden behind . . . an ambiguity" and may only be brought to light through interpretation.

Delusions and Dreams in Jensen's Gradiva revolves around a question of authority: who has understood the nature of dreams, so-called science or psychoanalysis? In order to substantiate the findings of psychoanalysis, Freud invokes the authority of literature. In so doing, however, he runs up against a problem, for the agreement between the psychoanalyst and the poet is not immediately obvious. *Does* the poet in fact confirm the psychoanalytic dream theory? It could be argued that the poet, in the controversy between science and psychoanalysis, supports neither one nor the other side—or supports both sides: "A strictly critical eye might object that writers take their stand neither for nor against particular dreams having a psychical meaning," admits Freud (pp. 8–9). "If only this support given by writers in favour of dreams having a meaning were less ambiguous!" (p. 8). Freud thus faces a task not unlike that of Zoe: he must transcribe the ambiguities of the text into unequivocal statements, arguing that such a transcription of the narrative into the language of medical psychology nevertheless preserves the essential meaning and content of the narrative.

Gradiva is a story about interpretation; yet this story itself demands an interpretation. The dreams represented in *Gradiva* are "not self-explanatory" (p. 57); in order to interpret these dreams Freud must borrow heavily from psychoanalytic (dream) theory. At the same time the very purpose of his essay compels him to claim that his interpretation has found nothing in the text not already there, hidden behind that which is ambiguous or apparently arbitrary. For if Jensen's novel, in the controversy between science and psychoanalysis, is to occupy the place of the ally of psychoanalysis, it must be shown that psychoanalysis and literature both understand the unconscious in the same way, and that the psychoanalyst and the author of *Gradiva*, independent of each other, have reached the same results. It must be argued, therefore, that both the psychoanalyst and the author say the same thing, although they express themselves differently.

Commenting on Freud's brief analysis in *The Interpretation of Dreams* of Shakespeare's *Hamlet*, Meredith Anne Skura points out that "Freud saw himself restating in scientific language what the poets were able to express only in displaced and distorted form. He saw only two poles of expression: that which was outright and scientific, like his own diagnostic case histories; and that which was repressed and distorted by subjective fantasy."[7] This characterization of psychoanalytic interpretation seems indeed to apply to Freud's own understanding of his reading of *Gradiva*. "We shall now reproduce it," he says, "with the technical terminology of our science" (p. 44). But between the poles Skura has outlined—between Jensen's "genuine poetical material" and the restating of this material in the technical language of psychoanalysis—a connecting link has been inserted. Commenting on his analysis, Freud maintains, "I myself have supported all the views that I have here extracted from Jensen's *Gradiva* and stated in technical terms" (p. 53). That which is translated into the technical terms of psychoanalysis is the content, "the views," he has "extracted"—in other words, the summary of the novel rather than *Gradiva* itself. Like Zoe, Freud has divided his treatment into two distinct parts, and it appears that his strategy serves a similar purpose.

In introducing his summary, Freud stresses that it is intended for those readers who are already acquainted with Jensen's novel: "But for the benefit of those who have already read *Gradiva* I will recall the substance of the story in a brief summary; and I shall count upon their memory to restore to it all the charm of which this treatment will deprive it" (p. 10). It is therefore somewhat surprising that his paraphrase takes the form of a first-time reading of the novel. However, the advantages of a naïve reading are obvious. Following the plot closely and pretending not to know how the story will develop, Freud finds the occasion to intersperse his summary with commentaries that prepare the ground for the interpretation to follow. Indeed, summarizing *is* preliminary interpretation; the paraphrase is a "stealthily appropriative reading"[8] of Jensen's text. Freud indirectly admits to this fact as he, at the beginning of the second chapter, looks back on the summary. It is so easy, he says, "to read meaning into things. Is it not . . . we who have slipped into this charming poetic story a secret meaning very far from its author's intentions?" (p. 43) The summary has brought out a "secret meaning" the author himself might not recognize. Thus paraphrase is interpretation, but is it also "tendentious interpretation"? We have tried, says Freud, to save ourselves from this allegation "by giving the story almost entirely in the author's own words" (p. 43). The text itself is called upon to confirm the faithfulness of the paraphrase. At this point, however, it has become clear that he has used the author's words as Zoe has used Norbert's symbolism: not in order to recapitulate, but to uncover a hidden intention. But the implication is that he, no less than Zoe, has preserved the substance of Jensen's "Fantasy"; he has found nothing in the text that is not already there.

Sarah Kofman has discussed at length this procedure of interpreting a summary of the text rather than the text itself. In summarizing Jensen's narrative, Freud dissociates its content ("substance") from its form ("charm"); is not this dissociation inconsistent with the principles of psychoanalytic interpretation, according to which even marginal features must be taken into consideration? "L'originalité de la méthode freudienne ne réside-t-elle pas dans l'importance accordée aux moindres détails?"[9] But if Freud's interpretive procedure seems to depart from psychoanalytic hermeneutics, as outlined in *The Interpretation of Dreams,* for instance, it is nevertheless in accordance with his idea of art.

As we know, art and literature were important to the founder of psychoanalysis. The references to literary and dramatic works that appear everywhere in his writings testify to the wide range of his literary interests. But, as Philip Rieff has pointed out, Freud also "inherited a good deal of that hostility to art which has accompanied the scientific attitude so long as it has been empirical in its pretension and practical in its orientation"; for the work of art *as such,* he "cared very little."[10] In "The Moses of Michelangelo" Freud makes his position quite clear. "I am no connoisseur in art," he writes.

> I have often observed that the subject-matter of works of art has a stronger attraction for me than their formal and technical qualities, though to the artist their value lies first and foremost in these latter. I am unable rightly to appreciate many of the methods used and the effects obtained in art.

"I must," he continues, "find out the meaning and content [den Sinn und Inhalt] of what is represented in his work; I must, in other words, be able to *interpret* it."[11] It is this understanding of the work of art that forms the basis of Freudian aesthetical theory.

Two years before the appearance of *Delusions and Dreams in Jensen's Gradiva*, Freud had published *Jokes and Their Relation to the Unconscious*, a study, in light of psychoanalytic dream theory, of the technique and purposes of jokes. The interpretive procedure adopted in this work has as its basis the idea of a clear-cut distinction between the "form" or "technique" of a joke and the "thought" it expresses. Translated into another linguistic form, deprived of its particular form of expression, the joke loses its power to cause a laugh; the form or expressive technique of the joke thus appears to be its essence.

Having examined in detail the expressive technique of the joke, which he compares with the expressive technique of the dream, Freud goes on to propose a distinction between, on the one hand, jokes that are an end in themselves, "innocent" jokes, and, on the other hand, jokes that have an aim, "tendentious" jokes. The tendentious joke achieves a deeper effect than the innocent, and since the technique of both is the same, the effect of the tendentious joke must depend on its content: "tendentious jokes, by virtue of their purpose, must have sources of pleasure at their disposal to which innocent jokes have no access." Now the purposes of jokes are easily reviewed, Freud continues, for they are either hostile or obscene. Tendentious jokes express thoughts that satisfy aggressive or libidinous impulses, which would otherwise have been suppressed. The function of the joke technique is consequently to "evade restrictions and open sources of pleasure that have become inaccessible."

> A possibility of generating pleasure supervenes in a situation in which another possibility of pleasure is obstructed so that, as far as the latter alone is concerned, no pleasure would arise. The result is a generation of pleasure far greater than that offered by the supervening possibility. This has acted, as it were, as an *incentive bonus*; with the assistance of the offer of a small amount of pleasure, a much greater one, which would otherwise have been hard to achieve, has been gained. I have good reason to suspect that this principle corresponds with an arrangement that holds good in many widely separated departments of mental life and it will, I think, be expedient to describe the pleasure that serves to initiate the large release of pleasure as "fore-pleasure," and the principle as the "fore-pleasure principle."[12]

On the one hand, the "form" of the joke is essential, since without its particular form of expression it would not achieve its effect; form is fore-pleasure, which initiates an otherwise impossible pleasure. On the other hand, the form is secondary, since it is merely the garb of a pre-existing "thought," the substance of the joke, which may be extracted and treated separately. In "Creative Writers and Day-Dreaming," published in 1908, a year after *Delusions and Dreams*, Freud applies this model of the tendentious joke to the fictional text. "The writer," he says,

> bribes us by the purely formal—that is, aesthetic—yield of pleasure which he offers us in the presentation of his phantasies. We give the name of an *incentive bonus* or a *fore-pleasure*, to a yield of pleasure such as this, which is offered to us so as to make possible the release of still greater pleasure arising from deeper psychical sources.[13]

Freud's summary of *Gradiva* should be read in this context. Summarizing is the act by which the text is stripped of its aesthetical garments. The outcome of this procedure is a text that lacks the power to please or to "charm" the reader, but which is claimed to be closer to the primary, undistorted content of the narrative, that is, for example, closer to the original version of Jensen's fantasy.

Nevertheless, the allegation of having read meaning into the text continues to haunt Freud's argument. On the last pages of *Delusions and Dreams in Jensen's* Gradiva, he brings up the question of the status of the psychoanalytic insight his analysis has revealed. It is quite possible, he admits, that Wilhelm Jensen may "repudiate all the purposes we have recognized in his work" (p. 91). If this is the case, there are only two possible explanations. One is that the interpreter himself has read these purposes into the text. This explanation would of course entirely undermine the purpose of Freud's essay. The remaining alternative is, then, that the author of *Gradiva* possesses a knowledge he himself does not consciously recognize; like his hero, Jensen does not know what he knows.

> Our opinion is that the author need have known nothing of these rules and purposes, so that he could disavow them in good faith, but that nevertheless we have not discovered anything in his work that is not already in it. We probably draw from the same source and work upon the same object, each of us by another method. And the agreement of our results seems to guarantee that we have

both worked correctly. Our procedure consists in the conscious observation of abnormal mental processes in other people so as to be able to elicit and announce their laws. The author no doubt proceeds differently. He directs his attention to the unconscious in his own mind, he listens to its possible developments and lends them artistic expression instead of suppressing them by conscious criticism. Thus he experiences from himself what we learn from others—the laws which the activities of the unconscious must obey. But he need not state these laws, nor even be clearly aware of them; as a result of the tolerance of his intelligence, they are incorporated within his creations. (pp. 91–92)

In the course of his reading, Freud has more than once inter-rupted his argument in order to praise the remarkable psychoanalytic insight he has found in *Gradiva*. Each of these expressions of wonder, however, seems to be designed to prepare the reader for the conclusion that the nature of Jensen's astonishing insight is entirely different from the psychoanalyst's. Having summarized the narrative, Freud remarks that although the author "has expressly renounced the portrayal of reality by calling his story a 'phantasy' . . . all his descriptions are so faithfully copied from reality" that he would not object if *Gradiva* were described as a "psychiatric study" (p. 41). In the same paragraph, how-ever, he points out that the artist's mind, rather than being "an ab-solutely transparent medium," is "a refractive" and "obscuring" prism. The idea of *mimesis* is complicated by the introduction of the author's "mind" as that which mediates "reality." Perhaps *Gradiva* owes its real-ism, not to its author's conscious observation and description of a reality outside himself, but to the fact that he has faithfully expressed his own inner reality? Perhaps Jensen has no conscious knowledge of what he is doing? "How was it," asks Freud, "that the author arrived at the same knowledge as the doctor—or at least *behaved as though* he possessed the same knowledge?" (p. 54; my italics). Is the process of writing perhaps determined by forces other than the author's arbitrary choice?

The final pages of Freud's essay propose an answer to all these questions. Psychoanalytic knowledge is differentiated from poetical knowledge of the mind. While the analyst derives his insight from "conscious observation" of mental processes in "other people," the writer penetrates into the "unconscious in his own mind." The "laws" of the unconscious, of which psychoanalysis provides a systematic description, are the laws the author has unconsciously explored and couched in poetical garments—indeed, they are the laws the creative process obeys. Consequently, Jensen has written a psychoanalytic novel he himself is unable to read. The author's psychoanalytic knowledge must be returned to him from without; it can only emerge through (psychoanalytic) interpretation. *Gradiva* is thus dependent on the hermeneutical power of psychoanalysis in much the same way as Norbert is dependent on Zoe. The author may indeed know a "whole host of things between heaven and earth"; his narrative may convey an accurate psychoanalytic insight. But to the extent that this knowledge is hidden in the text and unrecognized, even by its author, it takes an analyst to show that what appears to be a fantasy may, in fact, be described as a "psychiatric study."

On the one hand, Freud disavows an intentional reading of *Gradiva*, that is to say, he disputes the writer's authority; Jensen is not the privileged reader of his own creation. On the other hand, no clear distinction is made between the work and its author: the (hidden) knowledge of *Gradiva* is, somehow, Jensen's (unconscious) knowledge. The source of the work is the unconscious in its author's mind. In his postscript to the second edition, Freud attempts to pin down the "material of impressions and memories" from which *Gradiva* has emerged. A friend, he says, has drawn attention to two of Jensen's other short stories "which might stand in a genetic relation to *Gradiva*, as preliminary studies or early attempts at a satisfactory poetical solution of the same problem in the psychology of love." Proposing a distinction between the "manifest content" of these stories and their "latent meaning," Freud concludes that it "is easy to see that all three stories treat of the same theme: the development of a love . . . as an after-effect of an intimate association in childhood of a brother-and-sister kind."[14]

The source of *Gradiva* may be an allegedly repressed childhood memory of an erotic, perhaps even incestuous, association. But in fact, this hypothetical reconstruction has already emerged from the psychoanalytic case study Freud has extracted from the novel. Although he does not recognize the fact, Jensen has given an accurate description of the processes of repression and symptom formation, as well as of the principles of the psychoanalytic process. Only on one highly significant point does the author remain silent: "Our author has omitted to give the reasons which led to the repression of the erotic life of his hero" (p. 49).

Jensen has induced us to read the marble relief the young archaeologist falls in love with as a substitute for Zoe, his childhood friend. Norbert's devotion to archaeology, however, could not in itself explain his forgetting of Zoe. Science "was only the instrument which the repression employed," says Freud. "A doctor," he adds, with a reference to the analogy between psychoanalysis and the work of the spades, "would have to dig deeper here" (p. 49). Nor is it sufficient to say that Norbert has repressed the memory of Zoe, for "we remain on the surface as long as we are dealing only with memories and ideas"; it was Norbert's "erotic feelings that were repressed" (p. 49). From a psychoanalytic point of view, Norbert's behavior is only comprehensible as an after-effect of "erotic impressions in childhood" (p. 47); only the assumption that Norbert's friendship with Zoe had an element of "immature eroticism" (p. 46) could explain his amnesia. Freud's treatment of *Gradiva* as psychoanalytic novel exposes a gap in the plot Jensen had constructed. In order to represent *Gradiva* as a case history, Freud has been obliged to fill this gap, to (re)construct the information, which Jensen has covered up, from the traces he has left behind. And the conclusion that is reached suggests that the analytical (re)construction of Norbert's association with Zoe is by the same token the (re)construction of the "source" Jensen drew from. The hero's inner Pompeii is, somehow, his author's inner Pompeii.

The purpose of Freud's reading is to detect the case story in the "Pompeian Fantasy." But it appears that this purpose is bound up with the purpose of detecting the fantasy in the case story Jensen has written. The analytical movement is from "Fantasy" to case story to fantasy—conceived, not as a circular movement, but as a descent into the deepest layers of the text. Behind the "Fantasy," seen as pure fiction, as the product of the author's unrestricted imagination, there is a perfectly correct psychoanalytic case story; but behind the case story, there is fantasy—a fantasy that is no less determined than Norbert Hanold's delusion. From this perspective, the young archaeologist is Wilhelm Jensen's alter ego. Or rather, the love story of Norbert and Zoe presents us with the fulfillment of its author's innermost wish.

> In his childhood Jensen must have been very attached to a little girl, possibly a sister, and suffered a great disappointment, perhaps through her death. Presumably the other girl had some physical disability such as a club-foot, which in the story Jensen converted into a beautiful gait; it was the sight of this on the relief that suggested the idea.[15]

A "happy person never phantasies, only an unsatisfied one," writes Freud in "Creative Writers and Day-Dreaming." "The motive forces of phantasies are unsatisfied wishes, and every single phantasy is the fulfilment of a wish, a correction of unsatisfying reality." Stressing the structural as well as the generic relationship between children's play, (day)dream, and poetic creation, Freud proceeds to propose the following formula of creative writing: "A strong experience in the present awakens in the creative writer a memory of an earlier experience (usually belonging to his childhood) from which there now proceeds a wish which finds its fulfilment in the creative work."[16] Thus *Gradiva*, it appears, does not merely stage the fulfillment of its author's childhood wish; Jensen's "Pompeian Fantasy" has also dramatized the psychoanalyst's formula of creative writing. The description Freud has extracted from the narrative of the birth of Norbert Hanold's delusion, his Pompeian fantasy, is by the same token the description of the birth of *Gradiva*.

The principal character of *Gradiva* achieves that which reality has denied the author: Norbert is reunited with his first love. But for Norbert the way to erotic consummation is through mental disturbance; in his case the fantasy grows into a delusion. As will be remembered, Freud, in his summary of *Gradiva*, describes the hero as one of those "whose kingdom is not of this world." A "division between imagination and intellect destined him to become an artist or a neurotic" (p. 14). Art and neurosis grow in the same soil, but represent alternative solutions, as it were; and the path the young archaeologist chooses brings him dangerously close to madness. Norbert, therefore, is not only the agent of his author's wish fulfillment; he presents us with the fate that could have become Jensen's, had he not been able to turn his fantasy into a work of art. In *Introductory Lectures on Psycho-Analysis*, Freud returns to this theme. An artist, he writes, is "in rudiments an introvert, not far removed from neurosis. He is oppressed by excessively powerful instinctual needs"—oppressed by powerful, unsatisfied wishes. "Consequently, like any other unsatisfied man, he turns away from reality and transfers all his interest, and his libido too, to the wishful constructions of his life of phantasy, whence the path might lead to neurosis."[17]

Freud proceeds to claim that there is a path that leads back from fantasy to reality: art. The "true artist" understands how to work over his fantasies so that "they do not easily betray their origin from proscribed sources."[18] He "softens the character of his egoistic day-dreams by altering and disguising it."[19] In so doing, he makes it possible for other people to derive pleasure from the fantasy; he enables others to derive "consolation and alleviation from their own sources of pleasure in their unconscious which have become inaccessible to them."[20] The overpowerful fantasy, which threatened to supplant real life, has been accommodated within reality in the form of a work of art whose imaginary world is sharply separated from the real world. The return to reality, which Norbert only accomplishes through Zoe's therapy, has, according to this model, been accomplished by the author through the writing of his *Gradiva.*

In Jensen's story of delusion and cure, it is Norbert himself who finally confirms the reconstruction with which Zoe presents him. Having listened to Zoe's speech of castigation, the young archaeologist presents the final piece of evidence: the name Bertgang means the same as Gradiva; Gradiva is a verbatim translation of Zoe's family name. The archaeologist who until then has been confined to a quite literal reading of his own fantastical constructions is now capable of perceiving their second—real—meaning. The tracing back of the delusion is now complete; cure is achieved as Norbert becomes a reader of himself rather than a text to be deciphered. This, Freud points out, "is just how patients behave when one has loosened the compulsion of their delusional thoughts by revealing the repressed material lying behind them." Once they have "understood" the interpretation offered them, "they themselves bring forward the solutions of the final and most important riddles" (pp. 37–38). Apparently, Freud sought to obtain the same kind of verification from the author, since he presented Wilhelm Jensen with a copy of his analysis, asking him for information about the source of his ideas. But Jensen had next to nothing to contribute and showed no understanding of the second meaning the psychoanalyst had extracted from his work. The author seemed "altogether incapable of entering into any other but his own poetic intentions."[21]

The impossibility of obtaining confirmation from the author is thus suggestive of the discrepancy between the therapeutic process (Zoe's analysis of Norbert) and psychoanalytic literary criticism (Freud's analysis of *Gradiva*). Freud's analysis of *Gradiva* does not bring any "cure"; indeed, if there is an analysand here it is the text itself rather than the author—the text that is, so to speak, cured of its own fictionality as it is translated into a psychiatric study. Consequently, there is no way to confirm the analysis except through the text itself. Psychoanalytic literary interpretation is validated solely by its explanatory power, by its ability to explain even those apparently marginal textual features other readings cannot account for. We find, says C. Barry Chabot, three distinct but overlapping standards: "self-consistency, coherence, and comprehensiveness." If

> psychoanalytic interpretations are to be judged adequate, they must, first, avoid making contradictory statements; second, they must draw our understanding into a coherent whole; and third,

they must account for as much of the data, especially the odd and discordant, as possible. . . . Ideally nothing whatever would remain outside its orderly accounting.[22]

The interpretation is correct when it dissolves apparent inconsistencies, fills in all gaps, and arrives at a "singular solution" that accounts for everything and precludes "alternative solution[s]."[23]

At the very basis of Freudian hermeneutics we find the idea that everything is semiotic and thus subject to interpretation. As Philip Rieff has it, Freud "dared to assume that everything can be explained."[24] Everything can be explained, because everything is determined. Indeed, the underlying premise of Freud's argument in *Delusions and Dreams in Jensen's* Gradiva is the assumption that what appears to be chance may ultimately be resolved into law. In psychoanalysis, arbitrariness is but a law that has not yet been divined. "There is far less freedom and arbitrariness in mental life . . . than we are inclined to assume— there may even be none at all," writes Freud; "what we call arbitrariness in the mind rests upon laws, which we are only now beginning dimly to suspect" (p. 9). Far from being "unrestrained and unregulated structures" (p. 9), dreams are completely lawful mental products which, once their "syntactic laws" have been understood, may be translated into intelligible statements.

This, too, applies to the work of creative writers. Far from being the product of the author's arbitrary decision, the text is determined by psychic forces the writer does not control. If the dreams embedded in Jensen's narrative can be examined with the methods of psychoanalysis, it is not because the author has consciously imitated the structure of actual dreams, but because his imagination is itself submitted to the laws psychoanalysis has elicited. The psychoanalytic theory of creative writing leaves no room for the author's arbitrary choice and no room for chance. Everything is lawful and, consequently, subject to analysis.

In his discussion of Freudian hermeneutics, Paul Ricoeur has stated that analysis is believed to capture a reality just as much as does archaeology. A psychoanalytic interpretation, he says,

> finally runs up against an ultimate core where it stops. This is the sense in which I understand what Freud says about terminable analysis. At a certain point the analysis terminates *itself*, because it ends with *these* signifiers and not those: the term at which the analysis ends is the factual existence of this linguistic sequence and not some other. . . . Interpretation is possible because it regularly comes back to the same signifying segments, the same correspon-

dances. . . . To the notion of the terminable must be joined therefore the notion of the finite order of combinations.[25]

But rather than running up against "an ultimate core where it stops," Freud's reading of *Gradiva* runs up against a textual element that forces it to swerve, at least momentarily, from its original course. Rather than terminating itself as it reaches the deepest layers of meaning, his reading becomes caught in a double bind that seems to preclude "terminable analysis" as well as Ricoeur's notion of the ultimate "singularity of meaning."[26]

As it turns out, here is one element that does not seem to fit into Freud's interpretive pattern. In his attempt to solve the puzzle, he is left with one piece that does not fit in with the others: the ancient relief Norbert has purchased shows an exact resemblance to Zoe Bertgang, not only in the peculiarity of the posture of the foot as it steps along but in every detail of facial structure and bodily attitude, so that the young archaeologist is able to take the physical appearance of Zoe to be the relief come to life. The narrative itself provides no clue to an explanation of this uncanny similarity between Zoe and the antique artifact. The reader's acceptance of this highly improbable coincidence is, as Freud points out, the basic premise of the story. The similarity between Zoe and the relief "seems to lean . . . towards phantasy and to spring entirely from the author's arbitrary decision" (p. 42). Thus the "premiss on which all that follows depends" (p. 42) appears to escape or even to resist psychoanalytic interpretation. But convinced that it would indeed be possible to show "once again how what was ostensibly an arbitrary decision rested in fact upon law" (p. 43), Freud attempts to "forge a link with reality" (p. 42) by means of an analytical construction:

> The name of "Bertgang" might point to the fact that the women of that family had already been distinguished in ancient days by the peculiarity of their graceful gait; and we might suppose that the Germanic Bertgangs were descended from a Roman family one member of which was the woman who had led the artist to perpetuate the peculiarity of her gait in the sculpture. Since, however, the different variations of the human form are not independent of one another, and since in fact even among ourselves the ancient types re-appear again and again (as we can see in art collections), it would not be totally impossible that a modern Bertgang might reproduce the shape of her ancient ancestress in all other features of her bodily structure as well. (p. 42)

As Freud has remarked, the similarity between Zoe and the relief is the basic premise of the narrative. As regards this point, readers are simply obliged to suspend their disbelief. The similarity between Zoe and Gradiva thus appears to be the mark of fictionality; it is the one feature that prevents *Gradiva* from being a "perfectly correct psychiatric study." But the "improbable premiss" (p. 43) on which Jensen has based his story is a sleeping premise; it comes to life only as Freud seeks to root it "in the laws of reality" (p. 41). The "total explanatory ambitions of psychoanalysis"[27] have thus raised the ghost of fiction. A daring maneuver, indeed. For as it turns out, Freud's reconstruction of Zoe's genealogy stands at odds with the psychoanalytic interpretation that frames it. By suggesting a kinship relation between Zoe and Gradiva, Freud is on the verge of overthrowing the basic premise on which *his* story depends, namely the assumption that Gradiva is "a distorted and inadequate copy" (p. 37) of Zoe. In the context of *Delusions and Dreams in Jensen's* Gradiva, Freud's explanation of the similarity between Zoe and Gradiva is indeed a piece that does not fit into the puzzle he believes he has assembled—and may even be a piece indicating an alternative solution that cannot be accommodated within his interpretation.[28]

As Freud's paraphrase points out, a misreading marks the onset of Norbert Hanold's delusion: his misreading of the Pompeian dream. Prior to this dream, the young archaeologist had reached the conclusion that the relief that fascinates him "had been created by the imagination or arbitrary act of the sculptor and did not correspond to reality."[29] In fact, it is the peculiar gait of the marble woman that seems to preclude the attempt to anchor the artist's creation in reality. No woman of the real world would be able to walk like that, the archaeologist reasoned; the Gradiva relief could not refer to anything outside itself. But after having seen, in the dream, the transformation of a real woman into a stone sculpture, he no longer doubted that the artist had used a live model. The relief had acquired a new meaning to him; from being merely a work of art to be admired for its own sake, it had become a representation of a woman who had died almost two thousand years ago. Thus the dream turned the ancient work of art into a memorial. "It was, in a way, a tombstone by which the artist had preserved for posterity the likeness of the girl who had so early departed this life."[30] As a consequence, Norbert transferred his interest and love from the relief itself to its supposed original, the Pompeian woman who was buried in the ashes of Vesuvius. Gradiva had become factual reality to the young archaeologist. And as he, in Pompeii, encountered a woman who bore an exact resemblance to the relief, he jumped to the conclusion that she was Gradiva, the original of the relief, who had returned from the land of the dead.

As we have seen, Freud (in accordance with Zoe) offers quite a different interpretation of Norbert's dream and of his delusion: the Gradiva relief does indeed represent a real woman and is indeed a sort of memorial, but the real woman behind the ancient work of art is Zoe, and not Gradiva. The transformation that takes place in the dream designates the transformation of the young archaeologist's first love object into an antique artifact. From the psychoanalytic perspective, Gradiva was a fantasy that originated in Norbert's repressed erotic feelings for his childhood sweetheart and, as Freud points out, Zoe herself essentially shares this view. The real meaning of the delusion was thus Norbert's love for Zoe. "Fräulein Zoe" was "the original of Gradiva" (p. 66).

Thus *Gradiva* presents us with two different readings of the same dream text and with different chronologies, one of which is revealed to be delusive or false. Yet Freud cannot account for the similarity between Zoe and the ancient relief without re-creating the figure of Gradiva, without re-creating the fiction the psychoanalytic reading otherwise has done away with. By suggesting that Gradiva is the ancestress of Zoe, Freud, curiously enough, lapses back into Norbert's reading; the archaeologist's reconstruction of the origin of the Gradiva relief is superimposed on Zoe's interpretation of the origin of the delusion. The very moment Norbert's delusion is believed to be unmasked—"Gradiva is no other than Zoe"—Gradiva reappears behind Zoe. The very moment that the truth couched in the archaeologist's "poetical representation" is said to have been plainly stated—"'Gradiva' means 'Zoe'"—the figurative reappears behind the straightforward explanation. To accept Freud's explanation of the similarity between Zoe and the ancient relief is to admit that the deluded archaeologist was in fact quite right: the woman whom he encountered among the excavated houses of Pompeii *was* a ghost, an uncanny repetition of ancient Gradiva. Freud is left with two opposing readings of Zoe. According to the first of these readings, Zoe is the original; according to the second, she is a faithful copy or re-presentation of Gradiva, her ancient foremother. Thus Norbert's Gradiva delusion was simultaneously a symptom, a metaphor for the object of his repressed desire, *and* the actual truth of Zoe.

The double reading of Zoe therefore reintroduces the ambiguity that has apparently been resolved. Freud is once again caught in a double bind, caught between Norbert and Zoe, that is, caught between two epistemological models. By exposing the strange similarity between Zoe and the Gradiva relief, which is inexplicable within the context of the psychoanalytic explanation, Freud has torn the seamless web of his reading of *Gradiva* as a psychiatric study. His attempt to forge a link with reality by means of a (re)construction of Zoe's genealogy invites us, therefore, to reconsider the premise on which this reading depends. In the light of Freud's construction, truth is no longer unequivocal. Norbert and Zoe each represent the body of knowledge the other must suppress. In order to see Zoe as ancient Gradiva, Norbert must have repressed the memory of his childhood friend. Similarly, Zoe—in order to do away with Gradiva, that is, in order to claim that Gradiva is in fact Zoe—must ignore that she herself is the ghostly repetition of the ancient woman, the return to life of someone who died two thousand years ago. Truth, or rather the latent truth, is then not a buried Pompeii that must be excavated; it lies on the surface, but as "other," as the truth of the other. Norbert's delusion reveals the latent truth of Zoe; Zoe's interpretation brings to light the latent knowledge of Norbert's discourse.

Freud's construction has thus redefined the relationship between the two main characters; it has called into question the assumption that Zoe has privileged access to the past, that is, the assumption that she possesses absolute hermeneutical authority. In *Delusions and Dreams in Jensen's* Gradiva, the relationship between Norbert and Zoe, I have maintained, ultimately comes to represent the relationship between *Gradiva* and Freud as reader of Jensen's narrative, or between fiction and psychoanalysis. Perhaps this relationship, as well, should be redefined in light of Freud's construction: the fictional text confronts the psychoanalyst with that which he must necessarily repress in order to read the text as a psychiatric study or as the emblematic story of psychoanalysis (as archaeology of the soul). The return of Gradiva in Zoe suggests that fictions are not so easily eliminated. Norbert is cured of his delusion as he finally discovers that Gradiva was nothing but the insufficient copy of Zoe: fantasy, says Freud, has been conquered by reality. As we have seen this replacement, in Jensen's narrative, of fantasy with real life parallels the excavation of the buried Pompeii. It also parallels Freud's bringing to light of the case story embedded in Jensen's "Fantasy," as well as his uncovering of the laws of reality in the story that appeared to be the product of the author's unrestricted imagination. Thus Freud's reconstruction of Zoe's genealogy has far-reaching consequences. Ultimately, it calls into question the possibility of a psychoanalytic textual archaeology.

Significantly, the textual element that Freud's reading runs up against pertains to the issue of "origins" and "originals," which is crucial not only to Freud's concept of psychoanalysis as archaeology of the soul which *Gradiva* is called upon to illustrate, but also to his approach to *Gradiva* as a work of fiction. According to the archaeological model of psychoanalysis, interpreted events are also original events. For Freud, the "secret meaning" (p. 43) he finds in *Gradiva* is in a way its original content; the laws of the unconscious psychoanalysis has stated are also the "source" (p. 92) of Jensen's fantasy. Indeed, Freud's reading of *Gradiva* may be described as a quest for origins. First, Freud is in search of the origin of the hero's delusion ("We would . . . be glad to know how such delusions arise" [p. 22]). Second, he seeks to know the origin of the author's knowledge of the origin of delusions, that is, to know the source of the poet's psychoanalytical knowledge ("How was it that the author arrived at the same knowledge as the doctor—or at least behaved as though he possessed the same knowledge?" [p. 54]). Finally, Freud "demands to know the material of impressions and memories from which the author has built the work."[31] His attempt to explain the similarity between Zoe and the relief, by suggesting that Zoe is the descendant of the woman who was the original of the relief, is part of the same quest. In this respect, the (re)construction of Zoe's genealogy is quite remarkable. As a matter of fact, it does not merely suggest that originals are always already copies: Zoe, the "original" of Norbert's Gradiva, is herself a "duplicate of the relief" (p. 70), or rather of the model of the relief. As Gradiva originates in Zoe, and Zoe, at the same time, is said to be the descendant of Gradiva, we are left with the paradoxical conclusion that the original is a copy of its own copy. Zoe gives birth, as it were, to her own foremother. Freud's construction thus precludes the attempt to determine a stable origin.

One might say that Freud, in his attempt to anchor Jensen's "Fantasy" in reality, by accident opens a gap between *Gradiva* and the analogy with archaeology that Jensen's narrative apparently dramatizes. Paradoxically, the piece that does not quite fit into Freud's puzzle is the Gradiva relief itself. Freud's translation of Jensen's novel into the "technical terminology" (p. 44) of psychoanalysis is in fact nothing but the translation of one figure (*Gradiva*) into another figure, the analogy between psychoanalysis and archaeology. But *Gradiva* both confirms and resists this translation. Oddly enough, this resistance pertains to the fact that Jensen took the analogy with archaeology too literally. Zoe is not merely Norbert's inner Pompeii, the object of his erotic desire who, figuratively speaking, has been buried through repression and who is dug out in analysis. In more than one way, Zoe is the return of the past. As Freud's construction suggests, she is, quite literally, an instance of the revival of antiquity.

Chapter 5

"The Sandman": The Uncanny as Problem of Reading

The most concise exposition of the basic ideas of what I have been calling "psychoanalytical textual archaeology" is to be found in Freud's essay "The Uncanny," in connection with his interpretation of E. T. A. Hoffmann's narrative "The Sandman," which it singles out as the chief literary example of the uncanny. "Hoffmann's imaginative treatment of his material," writes Freud, "has not made such wild confusion of its elements that we cannot *reconstruct* their original arrangement."[1] This observation, marking the beginning of a long footnote that gives us the "analytical version"[2] of "The Sandman," sums up the premise of traditional psychoanalytic literary criticism: the idea of an original text, distorted through the author's poetic treatment, but nevertheless still retrievable. According to this, Freud's analytical version of "The Sandman" is, by the same token, the "original" version—a text that exists prior to the narrative itself. Psychoanalytic literary criticism presents itself the undoing of the author's imaginative distortion and the reconstruction, from the traces left behind, of the "original arrangement" of the elements. The psychoanalytic reader restores the latent, uncensored version of the text.

As a reader of "The Sandman," Freud adopts an authoritative stance that reduces Hoffmann's story to an object of psychoanalytic knowledge. Analyzing is represented as a regressive movement from textual surface to psychic depth, conceived of in terms of a movement from obscurity and "wild confusion" to coherence and intelligibility. "Freudian method," claims Frederick Crews, "invariably turns up traces of themes that Freudian doctrine declares to lie at the roots of psychic life, and those themes typically subvert the intended . . . meaning of a text . . . and replace it with a demonic excavated content."[3]

This characterization seems indeed to apply to Freud's interpretation of "The Sandman." As the analysis proceeds, it is only the substitution of the manifest text with its latent, fantasmatic content that allows us to comprehend the quite unparalleled atmosphere of uncanniness this narrative evokes; it is only this substitution that allows us to account for those aspects of the story that seem "arbitrary and meaningless" (p. 232).

Yet the most striking insight of "The Uncanny" is Freud's suspicion that his analytical reconstruction has in fact failed to explain the uncanniness of "The Sandman"—indeed, his haunting suspicion that the uncanny is precisely that which evades textual archaeology. Taken out of its context and isolated from the theoretical discussions that frame it, the interpretation of Hoffmann's narrative is an instance of psychoanalytic criticism in its most reductive and dogmatic form. What is so remarkable about "The Uncanny," however, is the fact that Freud calls into question the basic assumptions on which his interpretation depends, as he allows himself to be haunted by that which his interpretation excludes. The major insights of "The Uncanny" emerge not from his reconstruction of Hoffmann's narrative, but from the analytical space, which is the space of encounter of two voices, psychoanalysis and literature.

"The Sandman" is an enigma Freud sets out to solve, but that which is enigmatic appears to be inextricably bound up with those aspects of the story that are set off by his reading—those aspects for which his archaeological reconstruction cannot account. The enigma lies in between, as it were. It is this "in between" that my reading will address: the space that opens between "The Sandman" and Freud's psychoanalytic interpretation of the narrative. The focus of my reading is the figure of the "eye" in Hoffmann's story—the eye that constitutes the point of departure of the psychoanalytic interpretation, but which at the same time confronts us with that which this interpretation ignores or excludes. In agreement with Sarah Kofman and other critics who have commented on "The Uncanny,"[4] I stress that what is dismissed by Freud as "irrelevant" (p. 230) to the understanding of the uncanniness of "The Sandman" is precisely that which has to do with the problem of fiction and fictionality.

This applies first of all to the theme of Clara/Olympia, or life-as-death and death-as-life, which appears to be bound up with the theme of poetic creation, and, secondly, to the role of the narrator and the narrative frame of the story. But what Freud has excluded from his interpretation of "The Sandman" returns, itself almost uncannily, in the theoretical framework of his reading, in the concluding discussion of the uncanny and fictionality which, in fact, comes to query his interpretation of the uncanniness of Hoffmann's story. As pointed out by several readers, Freud ultimately arrives at an understanding of the uncanny that calls in question the assumption that uncanniness derives from the latent content, uncovered by psychoanalytic interpretation. Indeed, he arrives at a definition that calls in question the assumption that the uncanny is an effect of content at all.[5] In the following, I explore the transformations Freud's understanding of the uncanny undergoes. My main intention, however, is to show how this elaboration of the theory of the uncanny problematizes an archaeological reconstruction of Hoffmann's text and thus gives rise to a new understanding of reading in psychoanalysis.

I am reading "The Uncanny" in light of *Delusions and Dreams in Jensen's* Gradiva and wish to suggest a particular structural similarity between Freud's essay on the uncanny and his reading of Jensen's "Pompeian Fantasy." In each case, textual archaeology can be shown to entail the suppression of the fictionality of the text. In each case, the problem of fictionality returns; it returns in the form of a textual element that evades analysis. Is it a mere coincidence, then, that Freud's chief literary example of the uncanny could be characterized as the uncanny return of *Gradiva*? Both *Gradiva* and "The Sandman" dramatize the disastrous confusion of the living and the dead, the real and the imaginary world, the literal and the figurative. Both tell the story of a young man (Norbert, Nathaniel) who must choose between two women, one living and one dead (Zoe and Gradiva, Clara and Olympia); and they both tell the story of perversity, associated with the fact that the imaginary takes precedence over that which is real and the dead take precedence over the living.[6] Toward the end of this chapter, I return to this quite remarkable alliance between *Gradiva* and "The Sandman." But let us first of all take a closer look at Freud's interpretation of the eye in Hoffmann's narrative.

There can be little doubt, Freud maintains, that the feeling of uncanniness Hoffmann's story arouses is directly attached to the theme that gives the story its name: the Sandman who, as we are told in the beginning of the narrative, throws handfuls of sand in children's eyes "so that they start out bleeding from their heads."[7] "The Sandman" evokes the fear of damaging one's eyes, which is a terrible one in children and in many adults as well. Psychoanalysis has documented that loss of eyes is a recurrent theme in dreams and fantasies as well as in myths and legends. It is the study of such fantasmatic constructions, continues Freud, that allows us to trace the universal dread of loosing one's eyes back to its infantile source. Anxiety about one's eyes is a substitute for the dread of being castrated. It is this "peculiarly violent and obscure emotion," excited by the threat of castration, that "first gives the idea of losing other organs its intense colouring" (p. 231). The essay's introduction defines the uncanny as "that class of the frightening which leads back to what is known of old and long familiar (p. 220). That which "is known of old and long familiar" in "The Sandman," then, is the castration complex; the feeling of uncanniness evoked by Hoffmann's narrative originates in the repressed anxiety of childhood, the anxiety of castration.

"The Sandman" stages the disguised return of the Oedipal theme which ought to have remained hidden. The basic assumption of Freud's interpretation is thus the idea of a "substitutive relation between the eye and the male organ" (p. 231). The manifest term (eye/loss of eyes) is supposed to derive its terrible meaning and impact from the latent term (penis/castration). Only the assumption of such a "substitutive relation" enables the reader to clear up the obscure and intricate pattern of doubling and splitting the author has constructed. In Hoffmann's narrative, the Sandman is the abominable lawer Coppelius, who threatens to tear out the child Nathaniel's eyes and who is apparently responsible for the death of Nathaniel's beloved father. And further, Coppelius is Coppola, the optician, who sets in motion the train of events that estranges Nathaniel from his fiancée, Clara, and ultimately leads to his destruction. Why is the anxiety about the eyes intimately connected with the father's death? Why is the Sandman a disturber of love? "Elements in the story like these, and many others, seem arbitrary and meaningless so long as we deny all connection between fears about the eye and castration; but they become intelligible as soon as we replace the Sand-Man by the dreaded father at whose hands castration is expected" (p. 232). The author's "imaginative treatment" has translated castration into loss of eyes. It has split the father imago into two figures: the good father who intercedes for his child's sight and the Sandman (Coppelius/Coppola) who tears out children's eyes. The latter is only symbolically a father, namely the "father" of the doll Olympia, who is Nathaniel's double, "a dissociated complex . . . which confronts him as a person" (p. 232, note 1).

To Freud, then, the eye in Hoffmann's narrative is a metaphor of sexual difference. The eye represents the male organ, the organ the Oedipal father threatens to remove. The preciousness of the eye and the dread of having no eyes, that is, the preciousness of masculinity and the dread of being castrated, are the emotional poles between which "The Sandman" is suspended and from which this story derives its uncanniness. The figure of the eye is conceived of in terms of the dichotomy of masculinity and castration (femininity), possession and lack, presence and absence. But if one reads "The Sandman" rather than just Freud's summary of the narrative, it becomes clear that this dichotomy of possession and lack does not wholly capture the complex workings of the figure of the eye.

Freud's interpretation of Hoffmann's narrative presupposes the existence of a latent content behind the manifest text; his reading has as its basic premise the idea of a disjunction between the textual surface and the psychic depths this surface hides and yet betrays. The figure of the eye in "The Sandman" is intimately associated with this question of the relationship between surface and depth and between appearance and being. It is, indeed, intimately associated with the problem of reading that is the main concern of this study. Situated on the borderline between inside and outside, the eye is the locus of the interaction of self and other. The eye is the medium through which one reads—or misreads—the outside world. The eye of the other is, in turn, the medium through which one recognizes—or believes to recognize—the soul or inner world of that person. We say that the eye is the mirror of the soul. In Hoffmann's narrative, this saying becomes ambiguous; the mirror is reversed so that one sees oneself as one believes one sees the other.

Clara's admirers describe her as "deep" and "tender." Her eyes are compared to forest lakes; "heavenly music" flows "from her glances, to penetrate our inmost soul" (p. 125). Yet Nathaniel accuses her of being an "inanimate, accursed automaton" (p. 128), a cold and insensitive creature with no understanding of the deep mysteries of life and poetry. Instead, he finds the profundity that he longs for in the yearning, loving eyes of Olympia which, to him, reveal an "inner world, full of love and deep knowledge of the spiritual life" (p. 138). But Olympia is a dead wooden doll. She is pure surface, a mirror in which Nathaniel sees nothing but the reflection of his own desire. Her soul exists, quite literally, in the eye of the beholder.

The diabolic "play with mirrors" associated with the figure of the eye—the confusion of surface and depth, of outside and inside, of the living and the dead, of self and other, of recognition and deceit—is the structuring principle of the narrative itself. "The Sandman" is a gallery of mirrors in which everything is doubled and distorted. Thus the fight between Coppelius and Professor Spalanzani over Olympia is a distorted repetition of the attempt, on behalf of Nathaniel's father, to save his son from Coppelius. The faces with empty sockets that the child Nathaniel believes to see in his father's study prefigure the eyeless Olympia. Nathaniel's death, accompanied with Coppelius's laughter, reflects the death of his father. The Sandman, Coppelius/Coppola, as well as Professor Spalanzani, are distorted repetitions of the father figure; Olympia is an uncanny reflection of Clara, who is the double of Nathaniel's mother; the fate of Nathaniel is linked with that of his father as well as with that of Olympia; and so on. True, Freud's reconstruction has explored this complex pattern of doubling. But the play of doubling, repetition, and distortion of "The Sandman" is far more disturbing and uncanny than this reconstruction suggests.

Doubling and distortion do not merely pertain to the story told, but also to the very act of telling that Freud has excluded from his summary. Thus Coppola's spyglass—itself a demonic eye—is associated with Nathaniel's poem, which relates the fantasy of Coppelius as disturber of his and Clara's love. Both poem and spyglass occupy the same space; and both produce the same effect. The "pain" it costs Nathaniel "to draw [Coppelius] with sufficient colour in his stories" (p. 127) prefigures the difficulties the narrator has in telling the story of Nathaniel, as well as the narrator's desire to "draw" the picture in his mind "in all its glowing tints, in all its light and shade" (p. 123). Is Nathaniel, then, the narrator's double, or vice versa? What is, in fact, the relationship between the narrator's desire and Nathaniel's desire, between narrator and story, between the act of telling and the story that is told, between "outside" and "inside"?

By effacing the narrator from his summary, Freud has prevented himself from asking these questions. Yet Hoffmann's narrative suggests that precisely these questions have an immediate bearing on the problem Freud sets out to solve, namely, the problem of how to explain the feeling of uncanniness that the story arouses. First, it is suggested that Nathaniel's confusion of life and death, of the real and the imaginary world, and of the eye and the mirror, may not be put straight so easily. Second, it transpires that the relationship between the supposed original and the distorted reflection is more complex than Freud is prepared to admit. What is suggested, ultimately, is that "what is unsettling, if not uncanny, about 'The Sandman' is as much a function of its surface as of the depths it conceals."[8] I shall presently return to these issues. At this point, I will continue my thematic reading of the figure of the eye.

First of all, let us pursue the dichotomy of eyes and "no eyes" or "lack of eyes" that Freud has recognized in Hoffmann's narrative. In "The Sandman," possession of eyes is linked with life and warmth while lack of eyes connotes death and coldness. Nathaniel does not understand that Olympia is a dead automaton, until he sees her face with empty sockets. Lack of eyes turns Olympia's beautiful face into a hideous mask of death: "he had seen but too plainly that Olympia's waxen, deathly-pale countenance had no eyes, but black holes instead—she was, indeed, a lifeless doll" (p. 141). Without her lover's animating glance, Olympia's hands and lips are cold as ice; her very body radiates coldness—a coldness that is described as a "horrible deathly chill" (p. 135). In contrast, Nathaniel's mother and Clara, the women of flesh and blood, are associated with revivifying warmth. Following Coppelius's attack, the child Nathaniel falls into a state of unconsciousness, a "sleep of death" (*Todesschlaf*); his mother's "gentle warm breath" (p. 115) returns him to life. Similarly, Clara raises her fiancé from the sleep of death that follows his encounter with the eyeless Olympia. As Clara stoops over him, Nathaniel feels "an indescribable sensation of pleasure glowing through him with heavenly warmth" (p. 142).

There is nothing very remarkable about this opposition of eyes/life/warmth and no eyes/death/coldness, and I should not dwell on the subject, except that the existence of this dichotomy in "The Sandman" constitutes a third term: one which destabilizes the conventional opposition of life and death as it blurs or effaces the boundary between the two. The static dichotomy of eyes and empty orbits is set in motion through the appearance of a special kind of eyes: detached eyes, bodiless eyes, so to speak; eyes that do not belong unequivocally to one character, but circulate between different characters. The critics who have dealt with "The Sandman" and "The Uncanny" have not, I think, made it sufficiently clear that the detached eyes constitute a third term that Freud's binary scheme fails to master.

The theme of detached eyes is of course associated with the doll Olympia, whose eyes are said to have been stolen from Nathaniel. But Coppola's spectacles are also bodiless eyes of a sort. "Pretty eyes," cries the optician as he offers his wares for sale, "Pretty eyes!" And he goes on to cover Nathaniel's table with glasses.

> A thousand eyes stared and quivered, their gaze fixed upon Nathaniel; yet he could not look away from the table, where Coppola kept laying down still more and more spectacles, and all those flaming eyes leapt in wilder and wilder confusion, shooting their blood-red light into Nathaniel's heart. (p. 131)

At the sight of the optician's "eyes" a great terror seizes Nathaniel. And yet, quite ironically, he purchases another bodiless eye, namely Coppola's pocket telescope, which eventually will seal his fate.

Possession of eyes is coupled with warmth, lack of eyes with coldness. As the passage quoted above indicates, bodiless eyes are associated with fire, flames, and "bleeding sparks, scorching and burning" (p. 127). "Circle of fire! of fire!" cries Nathaniel, as he sees Olympia's eyes—his own torn-out eyes—lying "upon the ground, staring at him" (p. 141). Fire, in "The Sandman," figures as an agent of fatal transformations, crossings, and reversals. Fire turns everything into its opposite. Hidden in his father's study, the child Nathaniel sees his father bending over a blue flame. The flame transforms his "mild features" into "a repulsive, diabolical countenance. He looked like Coppelius" (p. 115). Later, the father dies in an explosion; he burns to death in his study as he, together with Coppelius, is engaged in some strange experiments. "On the floor of the smoking hearth lay my father dead, with his face burned, blackened and hideously distorted" (p. 116). But "when, two days afterwards, my father was laid in his coffin, his features were again as mild and gentle as they had been in his life" (p. 117). Thus fire appears to be a delusive medium; in the glow of the fire, the good father resembles the wicked Coppelius. Or is it rather that fire affords Nathaniel a glimpse into his father's true—demonic—self?

According to Freud, it will be remembered, Nathaniel's father and Coppelius are nothing but the two figures into which the father imago has been split. Fire, then, is a fundamentally ambiguous force. So are, in fact, the bodiless eyes. "Spyglass" is the English translation of *Perspektiv;* and the ambiguity of this term is indicative of the equivocal quality of the bodiless eye. Is the pocket telescope, which Nathaniel purchases from Coppola, an eye that enables one to spy on that which cannot be seen with the naked eye? Or is it a glass, a mirror in which one sees oneself? Is the bodiless eye a distorting medium, or does it provide supreme insight? There are no final answers to these questions. In Hoffmann's narrative, the bodiless eye is a disruptive term that cannot be placed. The bodiless eyes are neither eyes nor no eyes— or both eyes and no eyes. They are related to insight as well as to blindness, to life as well as to death.

Nathaniel directs the telescope toward Olympia's window. "Never in his life has he met a glass which brought objects so clearly and sharply before his eyes" (p. 132). In this respect, the bodiless eye is the vehicle of perverted desire. For Nathaniel is a voyeur, obsessed with that which is concealed behind closed doors and drawn curtains. In his second letter to Lothair, Nathaniel relates how he has peeped into Professor Spalanzani's room. This scene is itself but a repetition of the traumatic childhood scene Nathaniel had related in his first letter. Driven by an urge to see the Sandman, the child sneaks into his father's study and hides behind a curtain. From his hiding place, the child sees his father and the awful lawyer Coppelius engaged in mysterious experiments. In so many ways this scene is the key to the riddle of the bodiless eyes and thus to the fate of Nathaniel. But what was it the child saw that night in his father's study? In order to answer this question, we have to read the scene through the grid of other, subsequent incidents, since the traumatic scene appears to be nothing but a primal scene, which, like the Wolf Man's primal scene, is only understood after the fact.

Peeping into Professor Spalanzani's room, Nathaniel sees a young woman: Olympia, Spalanzani's daughter. Her face is like an angel's, but her eyes are strangely empty, "indeed there was something fixed about her eyes as if, I might almost say, she had no power of sight" (p. 122). Only too late will Nathaniel learn that Olympia is also the offspring of Coppelius/Coppola. In the childhood scene, Coppelius pulls Nathaniel out from his hiding place and threatens to rob him of his eyes: "'Now we have eyes enough—a pretty pair of child's eyes,' he whispered, and, taking some red-hot grains out of the flames with his bare hands, he was about to sprinkle them in my eyes" (p. 115). This scene prefigures the fight between Spalanzani and Coppelius/Coppola that Nathaniel witnesses. The two men are fighting over Olympia, the automaton they together have created, "a work of twenty years" (p. 141). Coppelius runs off with the wooden doll; Spalanzani throws Olympia's torn-out eyes at Nathaniel, "the eyes stolen from you . . . there you see the eyes!" (p. 141). Taken together, these fragments form a pattern. The scene Nathaniel witnessed that night in his father's study was a scene of conception. Peeping through the curtain the child saw his father and Coppelius attempting to create life out of matter. The kind of life that is the outcome of such a process is Olympia: the "child" of Spalanzani and Coppola/Coppelius who comes to life as Nathaniel's eyes are inserted in the automaton. As Sarah Kofman observes, the eyes—or, I stress, the *detached* eyes—"sont donc, dans le conte d'Hoffmann, le principe de vie mais d'une vie artificielle."[9] The torn-out eyes engender an artificial, fictitious, supplementary life that is neither life nor death.

The curtain is a common metaphor for the boundary that separates life from death, the known from the unknown, or the natural from the supernatural. A glance through the curtain is a glance into that which ought to remain hidden, a glance into that which is—or should be—beyond human knowledge. What the child sees is his father, who has sold his soul to Coppelius, driven by the wish to cross the boundary between death and life, between the inorganic and the organic. Nathaniel's voyeurism is, then, a repetition of his father's perverted desire. His fate is tied up with the fate of his father. Both are driven by the fatal craving for that which is beyond; both are haunted by the wish to see and to know, the wish to penetrate to the secret of existence and to solve the mysteries of (pro)creation, of life and death; both are driven by the desire to animate.

In the case of the father, these wishes express themselves quite literally. In the case of the son, the craving for knowledge, as well as the desire to create life, has been displaced to the realms of poetic creation. He wishes, characteristically, to animate Clara with the help of the poem he has composed: "he felt that it must rouse Clara's cold temperament [es war ihm, als müsse Clara's kaltes Gemüt dadurch entzündet werden]" (p. 127). It is thus consistent that the son should be the one to accomplish, unwittingly, the task the father had begun. By looking at Olympia through Coppola's spyglass, Nathaniel animates her.

> Involuntarily he looked into Spalanzani's room; Olympia was sitting as usual before the little table, with her arms laid upon it, and her hands folded. For the first time he could see the wondrous beauty in the shape of her face; only her eyes seemed to him singularly still and dead. Nevertheless, as he looked more keenly through the glass, it seemed to him as if moist moonbeams were rising in Olympia's eyes. It was as if the power of seeing were being kindled for the first time; her glances flashed with constantly increasing life. (p. 132)

The animated automaton, then, is the point at which different lines of desire converge, the desire to create and to animate, both figuratively and literally speaking, and the desire for knowledge and insight. In Olympia Nathaniel believes he can find the answers he craves:

> To me alone was the love in her glances revealed, and it has pierced my mind and all my thought; only in the love of Olympia do I discover my real self. . . . She utters few words, it is true, but these few words appear as genuine hieroglyphics of the inner world, full of love and deep knowledge of the spiritual life, and contemplation of the eternal beyond. (p. 138)

This knowledge of the "eternal beyond" Nathaniel ascribes to Olympia is bound up with the insights that he himself has attempted to express in his poetry. Indeed, the "real self" he believes he finds in her soul is his own poetical identity—the self Clara failed to recognize.

The whole thing is, of course, an illusion. " 'Oh splendid, heavenly lady! Ray from the promised land of love—deep soul in whom all my being is reflected!' " (p. 135). As we know, these statements are both fatal mistakes *and* the horrible truth about Olympia. The soul of Olympia is an effect of mirroring; the depths Nathaniel perceives are the reflection of his own narcissistic desire. "You, you alone, dear one, fully understand me," exclaims the young poet, who believes his stories and poems come to life in the other, in Olympia's glowing eyes. But Olympia is not other. Her eye is a mirror; the life she supplies is the life with which Nathaniel's eyes have endowed the automaton. While Olympia seems to be satisfying Nathaniel's desire for recognition, he, in turn, is satisfying another author's desire for recognition, namely that of Professor Spalanzani, who has created a work of art—Olympia—that, in the eyes of Nathaniel, appears to be life itself. Nathaniel, who believes that his writings have enthralled Olympia, is himself being mastered and manipulated. Professor Spalanzani must also see his life's work perish. Coppelius/Coppola returns to destroy Spalanzani. Olympia's eyes are torn out, Spalanzani is disgraced, and Nathaniel falls into madness.

Thus Hoffmann's story seems to unmask and to denounce the quest for (forbidden) knowledge and mastery. The male attempt to cross the borderline, to penetrate into the mystery of existence, to kindle life is opposed to the creation of life, which the mother and Clara accomplish as they raise Nathaniel from his *Todesschlaf*. Narcissistic, perverse creation of automaton life or illusory life is opposed to the feminine power to create life, which springs from the recognition of the other. In this respect, the bodiless eye seems, indeed, to be a diabolic mirror in which everything is reversed, an instrument of fatal misreadings, of distortions and reversals, of the confusion of the living and the dead, as well as of the installation of a perverse preference for artificial perfection over real life. And yet the dichotomy of narcissistic creation and procreation, of the artificial and the real, of death and life is not the conclusion of "The Sandman." In fact, this dichotomy is nothing but another mirror that forces the reader back into the labyrinth of the narrative. For what remains so disturbing about the story of Nathaniel is that something has been launched that cannot be controlled and cannot be contained within a simple opposition of right and wrong, truth and delusion. The confusions, distortions, and reversals brought about by the bodiless eye cannot be undone.

According to Freud, the theme of Olympia—the theme of the confusion of the living and the dead, of the real and the artificial—cannot be held responsible for the uncanniness of Hoffmann's narrative, because "the author himself treats the episode of Olympia with a faint touch of satire and uses it to poke fun at the young man's idealization of his mistress" (p. 227). Indeed, the narrator's satiric stance is perceptible in the passages quoted above. But satire, in "The Sandman," is less unequivocal than Freud is prepared to recognize. Far from being an independent theme, which might be separated from the theme of the Sandman, the theme of Olympia permeates the entire narrative.

The confusion of life and death associated with Spalanzani's automaton is bound to be repeated, even after the truth of Olympia has been disclosed. Toward the end of the story, Nathaniel, who has been reunited with Clara, is enjoying the view from a tower together with his fiancée. Suddenly he cries out "wooden doll" (p. 144) and, apparently in a fit of madness, tries to hurl Clara from the tower. This scene is in fact the repetition in reverse of the scene of animation, that is, Nathaniel's animation of Olympia. From the top, Clara's attention is drawn to a curious object appearing in the distance. "Nathaniel mechanically put his hand into his breast pocket—he found Coppola's telescope" (p. 143). Freud, in his interpretative summary of the narrative, misreads this passage when he assumes that it is the sight of the dreaded Coppelius that brings about Nathaniel's final fit of madness. "We may suppose," he writes, "that it was his [Coppelius's] approach, seen through the spy-glass, which threw Nathaniel into his fit of madness" (p. 229). But it is not Coppelius, the castrating father, whom the young man sees through the pocket telescope; it is *Clara*: "Clara was in the way of the glass" (p. 143). And just as the spyglass once showed him the doll Olympia transformed into a living woman, so does the telescope now transform Clara into a dead automaton, a "wooden doll." When the truth of Olympia was revealed to Nathaniel, the young man fell into a state of madness. The same thing happens now.

> Clara was in the way of the glass. His pulse and veins leapt convulsively. Pale as death, he stared at Clara, soon streams of fire flashed and glared from his rolling eyes, he roared frightfully, like a hunted beast. Then he sprang high into the air and, punctuating his words with horrible laughter, he shrieked out in a piercing tone, "Spin round, wooden doll!—spin round!" (pp. 143–44)

A crowd has gathered below the tower, and from this crowd Coppelius suddenly emerges. Nathaniel stands still, catches sight of the lawyer, and with the words "Ah, pretty eyes—pretty eyes! (p. 144) he flings himself over the parapet.

The price of wanting to kindle life is death. But not even death can bring to an end the pattern of repetition that governs the narrative. As it turns out, Nathaniel's failure to establish the distinction between the living and the dead, the real and the artificial, is contagious. The reaction of the population of the small university town to the story of Olympia is emblematic of this effect. As it becomes publicly known that Spalanzani's daughter was in fact an automaton, a "pernicious mistrust of human figures" (p. 142) begins to prevail. A deep uncertainty overspreads and contaminates everything. From now on, all ladies fear being mistaken for dead wooden dolls—and all young men secretly suspect their sweethearts of being automatons. As Olympia is now being associated with mechanical perfection, there is no way of proving one's humanity except through artificial, mechanical, *im*perfections.

In spite of themselves, Nathaniel's fellow townsmen, one might say, inherit the young poet's perverted preference for the artificial. Paradoxically, then, Olympia was all too human, precisely because she was a mechanical doll. "It is all an allegory—a sustained metaphor" (p. 142), contends the professor of poetry and rhetoric. But an allegory for what? For the artificiality of human life? For the fact that life is smitten with death? In this case, Coppola's spyglass would not be the deceptive, distorting medium it gave the impression of being. The demonic bodiless eye provides an insight, though it is not the knowledge Nathaniel had hoped for. Nathaniel's fatal confusion of an automaton with a human being has revealed a horrifying fact. The crossing of the borderline between life and death has always already taken place; the opposition of life and death, of eyes and no eyes, has always already been undermined. As lifeless works of art are animated through projection, so is life itself marked by death. This, indeed, may be the content of Nathaniel's final mad vision. What he saw as he looked at Clara, the embodiment of life, through Coppola's spyglass was that which Freud, at this point in his analysis, is not prepared to see: the uncanny return of Olympia in Clara, the encroachment of the artificial on the real, the encroachment of death on life. What was prefigured in his poem had come true to him: "Nathaniel looks into Clara's eyes, but it is death that looks kindly upon him from her eyes" (p. 127).

Situated on the borderline between eyes and no eyes, (in)sight and blindness, life and death, the bodiless eye blurs or effaces this boundary. There is not life on one side and death on the other, but rather life-in-death and death-in-life. There is not insight on one side and blindness on the other. Rather, there is the absence of any stable and secure position from which one can distinguish truth from falsehood. The bodiless eye is a figure for this ambiguity or uncertainty, just as it is the figure for the impossibility of mastering the narrative. For Coppola's spyglass is not only associated with Olympia, Spalanzani, and Coppelius/Coppola's oeuvre, and with Nathaniel's demonic poem; ultimately, the bodiless eye becomes a metaphor for "The Sandman" itself. As readers of this story, says Freud, we perceive that Hoffmann "intends to make us, too, look through the demon optician's spectacles or spy-glass" (p. 230). And to look through this demonic spyglass is to be smitten with Nathaniel's fatal desire as well as with the uncertainty, the "pernicious mistrust," that is the target of the narrator's satire. Only when it is too late will the reader discover that Hoffmann's labyrinth of mirrors has numerous entrances, but no exit.

As several critics have pointed out, uncertainty plays an important albeit purely negative role in Freud's interpretation of "The Sandman."[10] In the first part of his essay, Freud cites the work of a certain Jentsch, who "ascribes the essential factor in the production of the feeling of uncanniness to intellectual uncertainty; so that the uncanny would always, as it were, be something one does not know one's way about in" (p. 221). From a psychoanalytic perspective, this definition of the uncanny is, at best, "incomplete" (p. 221). As it turns out, Hoffmann's narrative is called upon to refute Jentsch's theory. Having summarized "The Sandman," Freud maintains that "this short summary leaves no doubt . . . that Jentsch's point of an intellectual uncertainty has nothing to do with the effect" (p. 230). And he continues,

> Uncertainty whether an object is living or inanimate, which admittedly applied to the doll Olympia, is quite irrelevant in connection with this other, more striking instance of uncanniness [the uncanniness associated with the fear of being robbed of one's eyes]. It is true that the writer creates a kind of uncertainty in us in the beginning. . . . But this uncertainty disappears in the course of Hoffmann's story. . . . There is no question, therefore, of any intellectual uncertainty here. . . . The theory of intellectual uncertainty is thus incapable of explaining that impression [of uncanniness]. (pp. 230–31)

Freud, in his vehement rejection of any connection between uncertainty and uncanniness, is in accordance with a much later definition of the uncanny, by Tzvetan Todorov.

> An inexplicable phenomenon occurs; to obey his determinist mentality, the reader finds himself obliged to choose between two solutions: either to reduce this phenomenon to known causes, to the natural order, describing the unwonted events as imaginary, or else to admit the existence of the supernatural and thereby to effect a modification in all the representations which form his image of the world. The fantastic lasts as long as this uncertainty lasts; once the reader opts for one solution or the other, he is in the realm of the uncanny or of the marvelous.[11]

To Freud, then, as well as to Todorov uncertainty is merely a preliminary phase of the uncanny. For Todorov, the reader is in the realm of the uncanny as soon as he opts for the natural solution (the fantastic events are in fact imaginary events). For Freud, however, an understanding of the uncanniness of "The Sandman" presupposes the reader's acceptance of the supernatural as a basic premise of the narrative, the acceptance of the fact that Coppola really *is* Coppelius and therefore also the demonic Sandman. Freud writes, "we are not supposed to be looking on the products of a madman's imagination" (p. 230).

Significantly, Freud's rejection of the theory of "intellectual uncertainty" is based on his own summary of "The Sandman"—a summary that neglects or represses the narrative frame of the story, or narration itself. What is left out of account is the fact that "The Sandman" opens with three letters (Nathaniel to Lothar, Clara to Nathaniel, Nathaniel to Lothar) that most emphatically compel us to consider the question of uncertainty that Freud has rejected. For these three letters, which circulate between three persons (from Nathaniel via Lothar to Clara, and from Clara to Nathaniel), present us with two different or even incompatible readings of the same events, readings we (the readers) must, but cannot, choose between. In the first letter, Nathaniel, prompted by his first meeting with the optician Coppola, relates the childhood recollection of Coppelius and of the death of his father. "A horrible thing has crossed my path. Dark forebodings of a cruel, threatening fate tower over me like dark clouds," he writes (p. 109). Nathaniel is convinced that the optician Coppola is none other than the awful lawyer Coppelius. And Coppelius is the Sandman himself: the embodiment of a dark, demonic power, "a hideous, spectral monster, who brought with him grief, misery and destruction—temporal and eternal—wherever he appeared" (p. 114).

According to Nathaniel, the childhood recollections represent the terrible truth of the Sandman. But Clara, in her reply, proposes another and, indeed, more plausible reconstruction of the events of childhood. Coppelius and the father "were making alchemical experiments in secret." Your father's mind, she continues, "was filled with a fallacious desire after higher wisdom," and he, no doubt, "occasioned his own death, by some act of carelessness of which Coppelius was completely guiltless" (p. 119). Consequently, the lawyer Coppelius is not a supernatural sandman. And Coppola is not Coppelius. The dark powers have no existence except within Nathaniel's own self. "I must honestly confess that, in my opinion, all the terrible things of which you speak occurred merely in your own mind, and had little to do with the actual external world" (p. 118). If "there is a dark and hostile power, laying its treacherous toils within us . . . it must form itself inside us and out of ourselves" (p. 119). The dark, demonic power that the figure of the Sandman embodies is nothing but "the phantom of our own selves" (p. 120).

Thus from the very beginning, the narrative raises the question of point of view: Should we read the story of the Sandman through the eyes of Nathaniel or through the eyes of Clara? Is the demon other or is he a projection of forces within one's own self? Are we in the realm of the supernatural or are we dealing with phantoms of the self? What is real and what is imaginary? Does Nathaniel's childhood recollection account for what really happened? Or is truth rather to be sought in Clara's analytical reconstruction? Having posed these questions of how to read, the text introduces a third pair of eyes, those of the narrator. Though if we expect the narrator to provide us with the insight that allows us to distinguish between the real and the imaginary, between truth and delusion, we are disappointed. All that a poet can do, we find, is to present life as "a dull reflection in a dimly polished mirror [wie in eines matt gescliffnen Spiegels dunklem Wiederschein]" (p. 124). The eye of the narrator is nothing but yet another (distorting?) mirror that reflects the ambiguity of the initial positions.

Who is, in fact, this mysterious narrator who refers to Nathaniel as his "unhappy friend" and who cannot divert his inner gaze from the remembered image of the beloved lost Clara? Like everything else in Hoffmann's narrative, the narrator appears to be both and neither: both inside and outside the story he is telling, and neither properly inside nor properly outside. He is implicated in the story he is telling, and yet this story has no place for him. The death of Nathaniel seems to compel a sharp distinction between narrator and protagonist, but somehow the protagonist lives on in the narrator. Rather than being the voice of truth, the narrator is the voice of desire, and this desire uncannily reflects Nathaniel's wish to animate. By addressing the reader, the narrator implicates us in this desire.

> Have you ever known something that has completely filled your heart, thoughts and senses, to the exclusion of every other object? . . . And you wanted to draw the picture in your mind in all its glowing tints, in all its light and shade, and laboured hard to find words only to begin. You thought that you should crowd together in the very first sentence all those wonderful, exalted, horrible, comical, frightful events, so as to strike every hearer at once as with an electric shock. (pp. 122–23)

This "first sentence" cannot be found. Having testified to his desire for narrative power, which is also the desire to animate the reader, the narrator renounces authority. As it turns out, the letters occupy the place of a proper beginning: "I resolved that I would not begin it at all" (p. 124). The letters are the mark of the absence or the impossibility of a beginning. The burden of interpreting these letters is therefore passed on to the reader who, once again, plunges into uncertainty.

The reader is confronted by an interpretive problem, and this situation turns out to be a repetition of the child Nathaniel's dilemma, as he is presented with two different interpretations of the phenomenon of the Sandman. Well before the primal scene, the Sandman is present in Nathaniel's imagination as a fantasmatic construction, nourished by his childhood nurse, according to whom the Sandman is a monstrous figure who actually exists, as well as by his mother, who explains that the Sandman is nothing but a figure of speech. From these two explanations, or maybe rather from the space in between, from the failure of these two stories to coincide, springs Nathaniel's desire to solve the enigma of the Sandman for *himself*, to see the Sandman with his own eyes: "But if I, I myself, could penetrate the mystery and behold the wondrous Sandman—that was the wish which grew upon me with the years [aber selbst—selbst das Geheimnis zu erforschen, den fabelhaften Sandmann zu sehen, dazu keimte mit den Jahren immer mehr die Lust in mir empor]" (p. 111).

As we know, Nathaniel's testimony is not the unchallenged voice of truth. His account may in turn be opposed to Clara's interpretation. What is repeated in and through the narrative is thus a certain structure: the existence of two incompatible explanations generates the need for a third position, for a third pair of eyes, so to speak; but, as it turns out, the authority of this third position, too, must be called into question. The absence of a final authority seems to be due to the absence of a singular origin. In retracing the strange attraction the Sandman exercises, we find that it stems from the impossibility of determining the nature of this mysterious figure. As the generative principle of the narrative, the Sandman is from the beginning poised, as it were, between two different readings. In this respect, the impossibility of a proper, formal beginning of the story about Nathaniel indicates the absence of an unequivocal origin of the desire that so uncannily is transmitted from the characters of the story to the narrator, and from the narrator to the reader.

According to Freud, the uncertainty to which "The Sandman" may give rise disappears as soon as the identity of Coppola is established: Coppola *is* Coppelius. As it will be remembered, this assumption was first stated by Nathaniel. Clara's sensible reconstruction is thus wrong—indeed, it is a fatal mistake. For Clara has instructed Nathaniel to separate outside from inside, real life from the phantoms of his own self. It is this piece of advice that eventually induces Nathaniel to suppress his fear of Coppola's (bodiless) eyes and thus to purchase the demonic spyglass. However, Clara is also completely right. What Nathaniel sees as he directs the spyglass toward Olympia's window is indeed the phantom of his own self. "If we have willingly yielded ourselves up to the dark powers," Clara wrote in her letter, "they are known often to impress upon our minds any strange, unfamiliar shape . . . so that we ourselves kindle the spirit, which we in our strange delusion believe to be speaking to us" (p. 120). This, in fact, is a very accurate description of Nathaniel's animation of the doll Olympia. The uncertainty to which Hoffmann's narrative gives rise seems to be an effect of this ambiguity that nothing can dispel—not even the information that Coppola is Coppelius.

Uncertainty, in "The Sandman," depends on the impossibility of a single, unequivocal reading. The characters of Hoffmann's narrative are constantly confronted with questions of how to read. And these questions are passed on to the reader. For how should we, in fact, read "The Sandman"? Should we opt for a literal reading of Hoffmann's narrative, or should we, in accordance with the professor of poetry and eloquence, say that "it is all an allegory—a sustained metaphor"? Are we in the realm of the supernatural, or does the narrative demand a psychological interpretation? Freud's reading of "The Sandman" hints at these interpretative difficulties. Having summarized the narrative, Freud rejects Clara's psychological approach and opts for Nathaniel's supernatural reading. Passing on to another level of awareness in his footnote, however, he assumes an interpretative position that is in fact not far from that of Clara.

According to Freud, we cannot understand "The Sandman" unless we as readers accept the existence of the supernatural as a basic premise of the story. On the other hand, we cannot understand the uncanny unless we opt for a psychoanalytic reading. The dark mysterious powers are phantoms of the self: Olympia is "a dissociated complex of Nathaniel's which confronts him as a person" and Coppelius, the Sandman, is nothing but one of "the two opposites into which the father-imago is split by [Nathaniel's] ambivalence" (p. 232). Does Freud's division of his reading into interpretative summary and analytical footnote testify to his unrecognized reluctance to make a definite choice between the two "solutions" Todorov has mapped out? If this is the case, we may be approaching another definition of the uncanny, closer to Todorov's definition of "the fantastic," touched on above. Whichever solution we opt for, Hoffmann has already incorporated this solution in his narrative. There is no interpretative position safely outside "The Sandman." The narrative has already anticipated all possible readings—just as it has, indeed, anticipated all possible definitions of the uncanny.

Freud's Oedipal reading of "The Sandman" is based on a double negligence: the neglecting of the theme of Olympia (or of Olympia/Clara) and the neglecting of the narrative frame or of narration itself.[12] As we have seen, the theme of Olympia is in fact inseparable from the problem of the narrative structure and the narrative dynamics of "The Sandman." This is, first of all, because Olympia is the embodiment of the desire for insight, the desire for mastery, the desire to create, to produce life. In this respect, Olympia is bound up with the narrator's desire to tell and to animate through his telling. Secondly, it is because the uncertainty to which Olympia gives rise permeates the entire narrative. Olympia is a problem of reading for which there is no irreversible solution—a problem of reading passed on from Nathaniel to the narrator and finally to the reader. As I have suggested above, what Freud excludes from his interpretation is precisely that which would have allowed him to see "The Sandman" not as an example of the uncanny, not as an object of a psychoanalytic explanation, but as an implicit *theory* of the uncanny. From this perspective, his misreading of the final madness scene—that is, his confusion of the return of the wooden doll Olympia in the body of Clara with the return of the castrating father—is symptomatic: the theme of Olympia is that which does not quite fit in with Freud's Oedipal approach to "The Sandman"; indeed, it constitutes a threat to his wish to master the text and therefore must be overlooked, if not repressed or negated. This brings me back to *Delusions and Dreams in Jensen's* Gradiva.

In order to proclaim the author of *Gradiva* the ally of psychoanalysis, Freud must turn *Gradiva* into a psychoanalytic case story; he must, as I have said, suppress the fictionality of Jensen's narrative. The problem of fictionality, however, returns. It surfaces where one would least expect to find it, namely, in connection with Freud's attempt to show that Jensen's fantasy is copied from reality and that its enigmatic and apparently arbitrary elements are explicable manifestations of hidden laws. Freud's attempt to explain everything—even the improbable similarity between Zoe and the ancient relief—and thus to "forge a link with reality" reintroduces that which his interpretation has supposedly mastered. Gradiva, the ghostly double, reappears in Zoe; the imaginary reappears in the real; the fictional reappears in the case story. What is at stake here is not merely the return of the delusion of which Norbert has been cured, but the far more decisive return of the question of the authority of psychoanalytic interpretation. *Gradiva,* Freud's emblem of psychoanalysis as archaeology of the soul, returns as the ghost of fiction, because the story Freud constructs in order to explain the strange, if not uncanny, similarity between the work of art and the woman of flesh and blood calls into question the possibility of containing the work of fiction within the psychiatric study he has constructed. Maybe, after all, there is no perfect agreement between the story Jensen tells and Freud's archaeological account of repression and cure. Maybe there is something Freud's archaeological approach cannot exhaust. And maybe this something is fiction itself.

These questions, written in the margin, as it were, of *Delusions and Dreams in Jensen's* Gradiva, become a central issue of the discussion that concludes "The Uncanny." Having completed his interpretation of "The Sandman," Freud attempts to apply his theory of the uncanny to the theme of Olympia, and, rather than confirming his theory, the theme of Olympia induces him to reexamine the problem of the uncanny. We may thus say that the position of Olympia, the living doll, within Freud's argument is analogous to the role Gradiva, the marble woman, played in his interpretation of Jensen's "Pompeian Fantasy." The theme of Olympia is a disruptive force. Olympia is associated with the "uncertainty" Freud has so vehemently rejected, with death—or rather with life-in-death and death-in-life—as well as with the desire that is so compulsively transmitted or transferred. It is the theme for which Freud's textual archaeology cannot account. But it is also the theme his argument runs up against; the theme that brings back what he has excluded from his interpretation of "The Sandman," and which ultimately obliges him to reconsider his initial definition of the uncanny, as well as the question of what is involved in a psychoanalytic reading.

Having reached the conclusion that the uncanny effect of the Sandman pertains to "the anxiety belonging to the castration complex of childhood" (p. 233), Freud goes on to ask whether one can apply the idea of an "infantile factor" to other instances of the uncanny—and first of all to the doll Olympia, whom Jentsch has singled out as chief example of the uncanny. Now dolls, as well as the idea of *living* dolls, are closely connected with childhood life. In fact, Freud maintains, "I have occasionally heard a woman patient declare that even at the age of eight she had still been convinced that her dolls would be certain to come to life if she were to look at them in a particular, extremely concentrated, way" (p. 233). But, he continues,

> curiously enough, while the Sand-Man story deals with the arousing of an early childhood fear, the idea of a "living doll" excites no fear at all; children have no fear of their dolls coming to life, they may even desire it. The source of the uncanny feelings would not, therefore, be an infantile fear in this case, but rather an infantile wish or even merely an infantile belief. (p. 233)

In the case of Olympia, the infantile factor would not be the anxiety of castration, but a childhood belief, the belief in animism.

According to Freud's initial definition of the uncanny as "that class of the frightening which leads back to what is known of old and long familiar" (p. 220), the blinding Sandman and the animate automaton are uncanny not because these figures are strange and alien to us, but on the contrary because they are metaphors of or substitutes for that which is only too familiar (i.e., *heimlich*). The source of the uncanny is not the manifest element, the Sandman or the doll, but the latent—repressed or infantile—content this element leads back to. But while this theory seems to explain the uncanniness of the Sandman, it certainly cannot account for the uncanniness of Olympia. The enigma of the uncanny, which the detection of the dreaded, castrating father behind the figure of the Sandman seems to have solved, is doubled as it becomes clear that the infantile factor Olympia "leads back to" is a childhood belief that may even be seen as a wish fulfillment. The implication is that the uncanny has no unequivocal origin; the source of the uncanny is neither the manifest element *nor* its latent content. In other words, the "reconstruction" of the "original arrangement" does not enable us to understand the feeling of uncanniness that Hoffmann's narrative evokes.

The displacement from "infantile fear" to "infantile wish" or "belief" in the passage quoted above leads Freud to include additional instances of the uncanny in his discussion. Of these one may mention the theme of the double (the phenomenon of "doubling, dividing, and interchanging of the self"), the "constant recurrence of the same thing" (p. 234), and "our relation to death" (p. 242). Eventually, he will have to deal with the question of the relation of the uncanny to literature and fictionality. At this point in his argument, Freud has apparently concluded his interpretation of "The Sandman"; no further references to this narrative are to be found in his essay. "The Sandman" is, perhaps, present after all. In his attempt to account for the double, the phenomenon of unintended repetition, and death, Freud is confronted with themes he has excluded from his interpretation of Hoffmann's narrative. In this respect, the second half of Freud's essay may be read as yet another, in fact a third, reading of "The Sandman," which testifies to his increasing and ambiguous involvement in the story his Oedipal interpretation had supposedly explained.

The theme of the double has been treated by Otto Rank, who "has gone into the connections which the 'double' has with reflections in mirrors, with shadows, with guardian spirits, with the belief in the soul and with the fear of death" (p. 235). The double was "originally an insurance against the destruction of the ego, an 'energetic denial of the power of death'" (p. 235). Doubling was invented as a preservation against extinction of the self, that is, as a protest against death as a major insult to narcissism. Thus the idea of the double may be traced back to "the primary narcissism which dominates the mind of the child and of primitive man" (p. 235). But, Freud contends, "when this stage has been surmounted, the 'double' reverses its aspect. From having been an assurance of immortality, it becomes the uncanny harbinger of death" (p. 235).

The double, therefore, seems to provide Freud with a clue to the otherwise incomprehensible feeling of uncanniness attached to the living doll. Like the living doll, the double was originally a wish fulfillment; the uncanniness of the double pertains to the fact that the primary narcissism in which it originated has been surmounted. What has been repressed (or rather left behind) is therefore not a piece of content but a stage of development. Every affect, says Freud, "belonging to an emotional impulse, whatever its kind, is transformed, if it is repressed, into anxiety" (p. 241). It must therefore "be a matter of indifference whether what is uncanny was itself originally frightening or whether it carried some *other* affect" (p. 241; Freud's italics). The uncanniness of Olympia, then, is similar to the uncanniness of the double. Or rather, Olympia *is* the double; and the "revers[al]" of "aspect," which according to Freud explains the uncanny nature of the double, is nothing but the reversal Hoffmann's story has mapped out: Inextricably bound up with the wish to create and to represent, with the narcissistic desire to find oneself in the other, and with the wish to master the mysteries of life and death, the doll Olympia is the emblem of the idea of the double. Olympia is the product of a narcissistic desire to reproduce life and thus to deny the power of death; she is the perfect doubling of life who returns as "uncanny harbinger of death."

It is obvious that Freud, at this point in his discussion, has already diverged from his original definition of the uncanny. Considered in light of the theme of the double, the living doll Olympia necessitates a reexamination of the uncanny. First of all, the theme of the double and the theme of Olympia suggest that the uncanny is not simply the "long familiar" that has been estranged through repression; uncanniness pertains to the *return* of that which has been repressed or surmounted. Freud's discussion of the double marks a significant modification of his definition of the uncanny—a modification, in fact, in accordance with the definition proposed by Schelling: "'Unheimlich' is the name for everything that ought to have remained . . . secret and hidden but has come to light" (p. 224). The expression "leads back to" is abandoned. Instead, Freud will define the uncanny as "something repressed which *recurs*" (p. 241; Freud's italics).

Secondly, the uncanniness of the double is inexplicable unless we take into account the reversal of aspect Freud has described, that is, the turning of the double as "assurance of (eternal) life" into its opposite:

"harbinger of death." It is suggested that the feeling of uncanniness, in this case, does not merely depend on the return of the surmounted, but on its return as other. Or, from a slightly different perspective, the uncanny does not pertain to the content but rather to the turning itself. In this respect, Freud's etymological description of the reversal of the term *heimlich* into its opposite, *unheimlich,* may in itself be read as a description of the dynamics of the uncanny.[13] And finally the reversal of aspect invites us to consider the context of the return of the sur-mounted. For it appears that the double returns as other, as "harbinger of death," precisely because it recurs where it does not belong; it returns in an alien context. The uncanny is a displaced return; the uncanny is that which is out of place. Uncanniness depends on a differential relationship between incompatible ideas. The uncanny, we might say, is submitted to the logic of deferred action; not simply because the double and the living doll only become uncanny after the fact, but most importantly because uncanniness presupposes a tem-poral distance or barrier between, for instance, primary narcissism and the stage of mental development in which the belief in animism makes its unexpected return—a temporal barrier which, to paraphrase La-planche, inscribes what has recurred in a different sphere of meaning.

While Freud's examples of doubles and doubling are taken from literature (Hoffmann's *Das Elexir des Teufels,* for instance), his examples of repetition and of "our relation to death" are drawn from real life, first of all from his own experience. A shift of tone is perceptible. The analyst has become his own analysand, as it were, and death, or rather the breaking down of the reassuring boundary between life and death, becomes an increasingly urgent theme. The distance between the in-terpreter and his subject matter has been reduced; the closer Freud gets to the uncanny, the more problematic does it become.

The factor of the repetition of the same thing will perhaps not appeal to everyone as a source of uncanny feeling, Freud admits. But imagine that one comes across the same number—"let us say, 62" (p. 237)—several times in a single day. (Freud was himself sixty-two when he wrote "The Uncanny.") "We do feel this to be uncanny. And unless a man is utterly hardened and proof against the lure of superstition, he will be tempted to ascribe a secret meaning to this obstinate recurrence of a number; he will take it, perhaps, as an indication of the span of life allotted to him" (p. 238). This instance of the uncanny—the forcing upon us of an idea of "something fateful and inescapable" (p. 237), which is irreconcilable with rational thinking—is related to the issue Freud will presently include in his discussion, namely, the return of the irrational belief that the dead haunt the living. But, in fact, the best example of this instance of the uncanny is not to be found in "The

Uncanny," but in *Delusions and Dreams in Jensen's* Gradiva, in the context of Freud's discussion of Norbert Hanold's belief that Gradiva has returned from the land of the dead.

> I know of a doctor who had once lost one of his woman patients suffering from Graves' disease, and who could not get rid of a faint suspicion that he might perhaps have contributed to the unhappy outcome by a thoughtless prescription. One day, several years later, a girl entered his consulting-room, who, in spite of all his efforts, he could not help recognizing as the dead one. He could frame only a single thought: "So after all it's true that the dead can come back to life." His dread did not give way to shame till the girl introduced herself as the sister of the one who had died of the same disease as she herself was suffering from. . . . The doctor to whom this occurred was, however, none other than myself; so I have a personal reason for not disputing the clinical possibility of Norbert Hanold's temporary delusion that Gradiva had come back to life. (pp. 71–72)

So Freud himself is in no way proof against the idea of the encroachment of the dead on the living; he is in no way proof against the delusion with which Norbert was smitten or against the "pernicious mistrust of human figures" associated with the theme of Olympia. The theme of the return of the dead in life, as well as the phenomenon of unwitting repetition, brings back the doubts his Oedipal interpretation of "The Sandman" seemed to have done away with, and this time they are not so easily mastered. Freud's discussion in "The Uncanny" of the unintended recurrence of the same situation and of the theme of the dead is laced with the vocabulary of Nathaniel's first letter: "something fateful and inescapable"; "secret meaning"; "daemonic character"; "presentiments." "The Sandman" has returned to haunt Freud's rhetoric. In some strange (or even uncanny) way Freud himself seems to have been smitten with Nathaniel's forebodings of the fatal power of that which is beyond, as well as with Nathaniel's wish to "penetrate the mystery [selbst das Geheimnis zu erforschen]."[14]

The phenomenon of involuntary repetition has brought about a further revision of the theory of the uncanny. The implication of Freud's discussion of the uncanniness of this phenomenon is that the feeling of something uncanny does not refer to a specific content or a particular experience, but to the repetitive structure itself: "it is only this factor of involuntary repetition which surrounds what would otherwise be innocent enough with an uncanny atmosphere" (p. 237). It is possible, Freud contends, to recognize the dominance in the unconscious mind of a "compulsion to repeat" proceeding from the instinctual impulses and probably inherent in the very nature of the instincts—a compulsion powerful enough to overrule the pleasure principle, lending to certain aspects of the mind their daemonic character. (p. 238)

We are now entirely within the realm of that which is beyond—or, at least, within the domain of *Beyond the Pleasure Principle.* The manifestations of a compulsion to repeat "exhibit to a high degree an instinctual character and, when they act in opposition to the pleasure principle, give the appearance of some 'daemonic' force at work." "But how," Freud goes on to ask, "is the predicate of being 'instinctual' related to the compulsion to repeat?"

We cannot escape a suspicion that we may have come upon the track of a universal attribute of instincts and perhaps of organic life in general which has not hitherto been clearly recognized or at least not explicitly stressed. *It seems, then, that an instinct is an urge inherent in organic life to restore an earlier state of things.* [15]

Here, Freud is on the verge of suggesting that the ultimate source of the uncanny is the death instinct itself. The uncanny is the drive toward the end (which is also the beginning), operating through the compulsion to repeat. It is true that Freud never quite abandons his first theory of the uncanny, but his new suspicion of an intimate relationship between the uncanny and the death instinct continues to haunt his argument.

"The Uncanny" is oscillating between two poles: on the one hand, the "uncanny" theory, developed in *Beyond the Pleasure Principle,* of repetition as primary event, repetition as that which overrules the pleasure principle, repetition as urge to return to inorganic existence; and on the other hand, the comparatively less disturbing theory (applied to "The Sandman") of a conflict between two forces, the wish and the repressive force. Does the feeling of uncanniness refer to the repressed, someway or other? Or does uncanniness have to do with the irruption of death or the death instinct into consciousness (or into the text)? In light of the new turn Freud's discussion has taken, we must ask: Does the uncanniness of Hoffmann's narrative pertain to the mise-en-scène of the threat of castration or rather to the perpetual return of the same? As we have seen, the characters are bound to repeat the same situation; repetition is the structuring principle of the entire narrative. What kind of desire is in fact operating in, or through, "The Sandman"? Is it a narcissistic desire, as suggested above, a wish to assure life by reproducing it? Or is it the drive for the end? Is uncanniness associated with the figure of the Sandman or rather with the figure of Olympia? And to further complicate things: Is Olympia uncanny because she is the double, the "insurance against the destruction of the ego," who has become a "harbinger of death"? Or is she uncanny because she is dead and inorganic—and has become an object of (narrated and narrative) desire, not in spite of but *because* of this fact?

"The Uncanny" does not provide us with a final answer to these questions, and the impossibility of making a choice between alternative solutions may itself be an important point of its argument. Freud's argument compels a return to the question posed by "The Sandman" itself: the question of how to read. We have seen how Freud in his definition of the uncanny expressly ruled out the hypothesis of "intellectual uncertainty." His discussion of unintended recurrence of the same and of "our relation to death," however, will lead him to include in his own argument the explanation he has rejected. Are we, he writes, "after all justified in entirely ignoring intellectual uncertainty as a factor, seeing that we have admitted its importance in relation to death?" (p. 247). Indeed, the factor of "intellectual uncertainty" becomes the primary concern of the final part of the essay, in which Freud, precisely because of the factor of uncertainty, will be obliged to consider the uncanniness of fictional texts as a separate case and, ultimately, to recognize that the uncanny has a privileged relation to literature or fictionality.

After having related and analyzed various instances of the uncanny, Freud arrives at the remarkable conclusion that he has not been able to solve the problem of the uncanny.

> It may be true that the uncanny (*unheimlich*) is something which is secretly familiar (*heimlich-heimisch*), which has undergone repression and then returned from it, and that everything that is uncanny fulfils this condition. But the selection of material on this basis does not enable us to solve the problem of the uncanny. For our proposition is clearly not convertible. Not everything that fulfils this condition—not everything that recalls repressed desires and surmounted modes of thinking belonging to the prehistory of the individual and of the race—is on that account uncanny. (p. 245)

The uncanny effect, then, does not derive from any particular content or subject matter.

For almost every example adduced in support of the theory of the uncanny as return of the repressed, one may be found that rebuts it. And, notably, it transpires that "nearly all the instances that contradict our hypothesis are taken from the realm of fiction, of imaginative writing" (p. 247). It is the threat of being castrated that "gives the idea of losing other organs its intense colouring," claimed Freud in connection with his interpretation of "The Sandman." "We shall venture, therefore," he concluded, "to refer the uncanny effect of the Sand-Man to the anxiety belonging to the castration complex of childhood." He now admits that not all fictional texts that deal with dismembered limbs are on that account uncanny. Fairy stories "are crammed with instantaneous wish-fulfilments which produce no uncanny effect whatever. . . . Fairy tales quite frankly adopt the animistic standpoint of the omnipotence of thoughts and wishes, and yet I cannot think of any genuine fairy story which has anything uncanny about it" (p. 246). The coming to life of an inanimate object and the reanimation of the dead have been represented as an uncanny theme. But again: "things of this sort too are very common in fairy stories" (p. 246) and therefore not in themselves uncanny. Fiction is par excellence the site of the uncanny, since, as Freud observes, "there are many more means of creating uncanny effects in fiction than there are in real life" (p. 249). Yet fiction is that which his argument incessantly comes up against; fiction is that which frustrates his attempt to arrive at a stable and consistent definition of the uncanny.[16]

We may at this point return to *Delusions and Dreams in Jensen's* Gradiva. Having paraphrased Norbert Hanold's first encounter with the apparition, which the young archaeologist believes to be Gradiva returned from the land of the dead, Freud breaks off his summarizing in order to comment on his own "bewilderment": "It is not only our hero who has evidently lost his balance; we too have lost our bearings in the face of the apparition of Gradiva, who was first a marble figure and then an imaginary one. Is she a hallucination of our hero, led astray by his delusion? Is she a 'real' ghost? or a living person?" (p. 17). Gradiva presents an interpretive dilemma; the apparition allows different interpretations between which the reader must choose.

In fact, the "bewilderment" which Freud reports recalls Todorov's definition of the fantastic: "An inexplicable phenomenon occurs . . . the reader finds himself obliged to choose between two solutions: either to reduce this phenomenon to known causes . . . or else to admit the existence of the supernatural." Not that we need believe in ghosts when we draw up this list, Freud goes on say.

The author, who has called his story a "phantasy," has found no occasion so far for informing us whether he intends to leave us in our world, decried for being prosaic and governed by the laws of science, or whether he wishes to transport us into another and imaginary world, in which spirits and ghosts are given reality. As we know from the examples of *Hamlet* and *Macbeth,* we are prepared to follow him there without hesitation. (p. 17)

"The Uncanny" should be read in continuation of this passage. For it now appears that the basic premise of the uncanny is precisely the impossibility of establishing a clear distinction between the real and the imaginary world and, consequently, the impossibility of choosing between different readings.

The imaginative writer, says Freud, has "this licence . . . that he can select his world of representation" so that it either coincides with the known reality or departs from it. "We accept his ruling in every case" (pp. 249–50). In fairy tales the world of reality is left behind from the very start. Despite their subject matter, fairy tales are not uncanny, for they are entirely set within the realms of the imaginary; we know for certain how to read them. The writer can also choose a world of representation that is less imaginary than the world of fairy tales and yet differs from reality by admitting supernatural beings such as demonic spirits or ghosts. "So long as they remain within their setting of poetic reality, such figures lose any uncanniness which they might possess" (p. 250). Referring, once again, to the supernatural apparitions in *Hamlet* and *Macbeth,* Freud points out that the reader adapts his judgment to the imaginary reality the writer has imposed on him: "In this case too we avoid all trace of the uncanny" (p. 250). For the feeling of uncanniness "cannot arise unless there is a conflict of judgement as to whether things which have been 'surmounted' and are regarded as incredible may not, after all, be possible" (p. 250). "Thus we see," Freud concludes, "how independent emotional effects can be of the actual subject-matter in the world of fiction" (p. 252). This statement, which marks a return to the surface of textuality, is implicitly a withdrawal from textual archaeology.

Freud's desire to explain everything—or, more specifically, his desire to accommodate the theme of Olympia within the psychoanalytic interpretation of "The Sandman"—has prompted a supplementary treatment of the uncanny which, rather than elaborating on his initial definition, has shown the archaeological approach to the uncanny in literature to be untenable. In his attempt to apply to other instances of the uncanny the hypothesis of an infantile factor, derived from the Oedipal reading of the theme of loosing one's eyes, he has launched an inquiry into the uncanny that once again confronts him with problems he believed he had solved.

In light of Freud's concluding remarks, the figure of the eye in "The Sandman" assumes a new importance to the theory of the uncanny. An uncanny effect, it is maintained, "is often and easily produced when the distinction between imagination and reality is effaced" (p. 244). Ambiguously poised between seeing and blindness, between truth and deceit, the detached eye in Hoffmann's narrative is the figure of such effacement. Situated on the surface, the eye is the boundary between inside and outside, self and other; it is precisely the collapse of this boundary that "The Sandman" enacts. As a vehicle for perpetual crossings, the eye—the detached eye—disturbs the dichotomy between life and death and prevents us from establishing a clear distinction between the real and the imaginary world. The eye, therefore, is the figure of the textual undecidability that is the basic premise of the uncanny effect—whatever its source in the unconscious may be.

Freud began his essay by presenting "The Sandman" as an *unheimlich* story which, once it had been analyzed, would confirm the psychoanalytic theory of the uncanny. But rather than being an object passively awaiting psychoanalytic excavation and reconstruction, Hoffmann's narrative turns out to be a highly complex work that offers resistance to the Freudian approach. The point of departure of the psychoanalytic interpretation was the assumption of a "substitutive relation between the eye and the male organ," and between the fear of losing one's eyes and the anxiety of castration. "The Uncanny" ends by showing that this assumption does not explain the uncanny effect. The interpretive pattern Freud applies to Hoffmann's narrative has already been undermined by the text itself. By constructing a system of binary oppositions destabilized through the appearance of a third term, "The Sandman" escapes Freudian systematics. On the level of that which is narrated, this third term is the bodiless eye, the telescope that generates the fictitious, supplementary life of Olympia, the life that is neither/nor and both/and. On the level of narration the third term is the third point of view, the narrator who renounces authority and thus disturbs the reader's expectation of a singular solution.

In the context of "The Uncanny," "The Sandman" is itself a disruptive term that problematizes Freud's archaeological reconstruction, as it returns to haunt his argument. But from the failure of Freudian archaeology something else has emerged: an understanding of textuality and uncanniness that belongs neither to Freud nor to Hoffmann, but to both.

Notes

Preface

1. Philip Rieff, *Freud: The Mind of the Moralist,* 3rd ed. (Chicago and London: University of Chicago Press, 1979), p. 105.

2. Steven Marcus, *Freud and the Culture of Psychoanalysis* (New York and London: W.W. Norton & Company, 1987), p. 18.

3. The models of such a close reading are Jean Laplanche's brilliant *Life and Death in Psychoanalysis,* trans. Jeffrey Mehlman (Baltimore and London: Johns Hopkins University Press, 1976); Sarah Kofman's Derridean reading of Freud's theory of art and literature in *L'enfance de l'art: Une interprétation de l'esthétique freudienne* (Paris: Payot, 1970), as well as her *Quatre romans analytiques* (Paris: Galilée, 1973); and Samuel Weber's *Freud-Legende* (Olten und Freiburg: Walter-Verlag, 1979).

4. Sigmund Freud, "The Uncanny" (1919), vol. XVII, p. 232, n. 1. Unless otherwise indicated, all references to Freud's writings are to *The Standard Edition of the Complete Psychological Works of Sigmund Freud,* translated from the German under the general editorship of James Strachey, in collaboration with Anna Freud, assisted by Alix Strachey and Alan Tyson, 24 vols. (London: Hogarth Press, 1953–1974). Hereafter: *Standard Edition.*

5. Malcolm Bowie, *Freud, Proust and Lacan: Theory as Fiction* (Cambridge: Cambridge University Press, 1987), p. 19.

6. I draw the distinction between "from" and "relating to" from Freud's essay "Screen Memories" (1899): "It may indeed be questioned," writes Freud, "whether we have any memories at all *from* our childhood: memories *relating to* our childhood may be all that we possess." *Standard Edition,* vol. III, p. 322; Freud's italics.

7. Donald P. Spence, *The Freudian Metaphor: Toward Paradigm Change in Psychoanalysis* (New York and London: W.W. Norton & Company, 1987), p. 7.

8. This study will not deal with Lacan. Lacanian psychoanalysis is, however, implicitly present in my argument, since it is virtually impossible to read Freud today except through the filter of Lacan's rereading of the Freudian unconscious.

9. Sigmund Freud, *Extracts from the Fliess Papers* (1950a), *Standard Edition,* vol. I, p. 233; Freud's italics.

10. Sigmund Freud, "Further Remarks on the Neuro-Psychoses of Defense" (1896a), *Standard Edition,* vol. III, p. 167, n. 2; Freud's italics.

11. Peter Brooks, "The Idea of a Psychoanalytic Literary Criticism," *Critical Inquiry* 13 (Winter 1987), p. 334.

12. Perry Meisel, "Introduction: Freud as Literature," in *Freud: A Collection of Critical Essays*, ed. Meisel (Englewood Cliffs, N.J.: Prentice-Hall, 1981), p. 2.

13. Theodor W. Adorno, *Ästhetische Theorie* (Frankfurt am Main: Suhrkamp, 1970), p. 506.

14. Sigmund Freud, *Delusions and Dreams in Jensen's* Gradiva (1907), *Standard Edition*, vol. IX.

Chapter 1. The Analytical Construction: Psychoanalysis and Truth

1. Sigmund Freud, *Leonardo da Vinci and a Memory of His Childhood* (1910), *Standard Edition*, vol. XI, p. 134.

2. See editor's introduction to "The Aetiology of Hysteria" (1896b), *Standard Edition*, vol. III, p. 189. The remark is ascribed to Krafft-Ebing.

3. Josef Breuer and Sigmund Freud, *Studies on Hysteria* (1893–95), *Standard Edition*, vol. II, p. 160.

4. Donald P. Spence, *Narrative Truth and Historical Truth: Meaning and Interpretation in Psychoanalysis* (New York and London: W.W. Norton and Company, 1982). Subsequent references to this work will be included in the text.

5. Wolfgang Loch, "Psychoanalysis and Truth," in *Psychiatry and the Humanities* (New Haven: Yale University Press, 1977), vol. II, *Thought, Consciousness and Reality*, ed. J. H. Smith, pp. 220–21.

6. My brief characterization, in the following, of "traditional" psychoanalytic literary criticism does not pretend to exhaust all aspects of that which is in fact a rich and diversified field of inquiry. I shall quote only from critics whose theoretical frame of reference is Freudian psychoanalysis. Within the scope of this study, I cannot go into a discussion of the kinds of psychoanalytic criticism inspired by, for instance, the works of Melanie Klein or D. W. Winnicott. Nor shall I take into account the contributions by ego-psychological critics, such as Ernst Kris and Norman N. Holland. For an excellent historical outline of various schools of psychoanalytic literary criticism, see Elizabeth Wright, *Psychoanalytic Criticism: Theory in Practice* (London and New York: Methuen, 1984). See also Meredith Anne Skura, *The Literary Use of the Psychoanalytic Process* (New Haven and London: Yale University Press, 1981), who suggests that the different kinds of psychoanalytic criticism derive from different aspects of the psychoanalytic process.

7. Quoted in Lionel Trilling, "Freud and Literature," in *Freud: A Collection of Critical Essays*, ed. Perry Meisel (Englewood Cliffs, N.J.: Prentice-Hall, 1981).

8. *Delusions and Dreams in Jensen's* Gradiva, pp. 43–44 and 92.

9. Simon O. Lesser, *Fiction and the Unconscious* (Boston: Beacon Press, 1957), p. 15.

10. Ibid.

11. Hayden White, "Historical Pluralism," *Critical Inquiry* 12 (1986), p. 484. The topic of White's article is the use of history in literary studies. I do think, however, that the lines I quote from White may also apply to the use of psychoanalysis in literary criticism.

12. C. Barry Chabot, *Freud on Schreber: Psychoanalytic Theory and the Critical Act* (Amherst: University of Massachusetts Press, 1982), p. 75.

13. Frederick Crews, *Out of My System: Psychoanalysis, Ideology, and Critical

Method (New York: Oxford University Press, 1975), p. 166. For Crews's psycho-analytic literary criticism, see *The Sins of the Fathers: Hawthorne's Psychological Themes* (New York: Oxford University Press, 1966).

14. Susan Rubin Suleiman, "Nadja, Dora, Lol V. Stein: Women, Madness and Narrative," in *Discourse in Psychoanalysis and Literature,* ed. Shlomith Rimmon-Kenan (London and New York: Methuen, 1987), p. 147.

15. Shoshana Felman, "To Open the Question," in *Literature and Psycho-analysis: The Question of Reading. Otherwise,* ed. Felman (Baltimore and London: Johns Hopkins University Press, 1982), p. 5; Felman's italics.

16. Ernest Jones, *Hamlet and Oedipus* (New York: W.W. Norton and Company, 1976), p. 13.

17. André Green, "The Analyst, Symbolization, and Absence in the Ana-lytical Setting," *International Journal of Psycho-Analysis* 56 (1975), p. 12.

18. Donald P. Spence, *The Freudian Metaphor,* p. 28.

19. See, for example, Elizabeth Dalton, *Unconscious Structure in* The Idiot: *A Study in Literature and Psychoanalysis* (Princeton: Princeton University Press, 1979).

20. See, for instance, her discussion of Edmund Wilson's dogmatic psy-choanalytic interpretation of *The Turn of the Screw* in "Turning the Screw of Interpretation," in *Literature and Psychoanalysis,* pp. 94–207.

21. Shoshana Felman, "On Reading Poetry: Reflections on the Limits and Possibilities of Psychoanalytic Approaches," in *The Purloined Poe: Lacan, Der-rida, and Psychoanalytic Reading,* ed. John P. Muller and William J. Richardson (Baltimore and London: Johns Hopkins Press, 1988), p. 148; Felman's italics. *The Purloined Poe* also reprints Lacan's famous "Seminar on 'The Purloined Letter,'" as well as selections from Marie Bonaparte's classic study, *The Life and Works of Edgar Allan Poe: A Psycho-Analytic Interpretation.* For a critique of Freud-ian "logic of representation" that tallies with Felman's critique of the sur-face/depth model see, for instance, Sarah Kofman's reading of Freudian aes-thetics in *L'enfance de l'art,* and Jean-Louis Baudry, "Freud et 'la création littéraire,'" *Tel Quel* 32 (1968), pp. 63–85.

22. Significantly, Spence's index holds only one reference to the term "unconscious." The reference is to his critique of Lacan's theory of "the uncon-scious as a langauge" (*Narrative Truth and Historical Truth,* p. 41).

23. Roy Schafer, "Narration in the Psychoanalytic Dialogue," in *On Narra-tive,* ed. W. J. T. Mitchell (Chicago and London: University of Chicago Press, 1981), p. 25. The "codes" or "narrative structures" to which Schafer is referring are parts of that which Jürgen Habermas calls the Freudian "metahermeneu-tics." "Theory," writes Habermas, "can take the form of a narrative." *Knowledge and Human Interests,* trans. Jeremy J. Shapiro (Boston: Beacon Press, 1971), p. 259.

24. Felman, "To Open the Question," p. 6.

25. Peter Brooks, *Reading for the Plot: Design and Intention in Narrative* (New York: Vintage Books, 1985), p. 270.

26. Peter Brooks, "Psychoanalytic Constructions and Narrative Mean-ings," *Paragraph* (1986), p. 53.

27. Paul Jay, *Being in the Text: Self-Representation from Wordsworth to Roland Barthes* (Ithaca and London: Cornell University Press, 1984), p. 25.

28. In *Freud and the Culture of Psychoanalysis,* Steven Marcus—who claims that Freud's case story is "a great work of literature"—analyzes the case of Dora "from the point of view of literary criticism," that is, "as a piece of writing" (p.

42). Other critics—Suleiman (see above) and Toril Moi—deal with the questions of genders, narrative, and psychoanalytic epistemology. Moi's essay, "Representation of Patriarchy: Sexuality and Epistemology in Freud's Dora," is reprinted in *In Dora's Case: Freud—Hysteria—Feminism,* ed. Charles Bernheimer and Claire Kahane (New York: Columbia University Press, 1985), an important collection that brings together a large body of recent commentary on the case.

29. Sigmund Freud, *Fragment of an Analysis of a Case of Hysteria* (1905b), *Standard Edition,* vol. VII, p. 16. Subsequent references will be included in the text.

30. Jacques Lacan, "Intervention on Transference," in *In Dora's Case,* Bernheimer and Kahane, eds., p. 101.

31. Marcus, *Freud and the Culture of Psychoanalysis,* p. 76.

32. Claire Kahane, "Introduction. Part 2," in *In Dora's Case,* p. 24.

33. Moi, "Representation of Patriarchy: Sexuality and Epistemology in Freud's Dora" pp. 196, 187.

34. Marcus, *Freud and the Culture of Psychoanalysis,* pp. 42–86.

35. Brooks, *Reading for the Plot,* p. 270.

36. Brooks, "Constructions psychanalytiques et narratives," *Poétique* 61 (1985), p. 65.

37. Brooks, "Psychoanalytic Constructions and Narrative Meanings," p. 55.

38. Ibid., p. 53.

39. Critics and theorists of different views have commented on this essay. Thus Jürgen Habermas cites it in support of his idea that "[t]he interpretation of a case is corroborated only by the successful *continuation of a self-formative process*" (*Knowledge and Human Interest,* p. 325), while Julia Kristeva, in her commentary to Freud's essay in "Psychoanalysis and the Polis" (in *The Politics of Interpretation,* ed. W. J. T. Mitchell [Chicago and London: University of Chicago Press, 1983]), explores the relationship between delirium and psychoanalytic interpretation. Finally, Peter Brooks has discussed this essay in the light of narrative theory in, for instance, "Psychoanalytic Constructions and Narrative Meanings."

40. Sigmund Freud, "Constructions in Analysis" (1937b), *Standard Edition,* vol. XXIII, p. 258. Subsequent references to this essay will be included in the text.

41. *Studies on Hysteria,* p. 7; Freud's italics. An almost identical expression is used in "Constructions in Analysis": The patients are "suffering from their own reminiscences" (p. 268).

42. Sigmund Freud, "Remembering, Repeating and Working-Through" (1914b), *Standard Edition,* vol. XII, p. 148.

43. Serge Viderman, *La construction de l'espace analytique* (Paris: Gallimard, 1982), p. 25.

44. Maria Cardinal, *Les mots pour le dire* (Paris: Bernard Grasset, 1975).

45. Spence, *Narrative Truth and Historical Truth,* p. 165.

46. "Remembering, Repeating and Working-Through," p. 149.

47. Sigmund Freud, *Moses and Monotheism* (1939), *Standard Edition,* vol. XXIII, p. 129; Freud's italics.

48. Spence, *Narrative Truth and Historical Truth,* p. 27; my italics.

49. *Moses and Monotheism,* p. 130.

50. Nicolas Abraham, "The Shell and the Kernel," trans. Nicolas Rand, *Diacritics* (March 1979), p. 17.

51. Malcolm Bowie, *Freud, Proust, and Lacan: Theory as Fiction* (Cambridge: Cambridge University Press, 1987), p. 17.

52. *Fragment of an Analysis of a Case of Hysteria*, p. 12.

53. Moi, "Representation of Patriarchy: Sexuality and Epistemology in Freud's Dora," pp. 197, 198.

54. Suleiman, "Nadja, Dora, Lol V. Stein: Women, Madness and Narrative," p. 147.

55. Felman, "To Open the Question," p. 6; Felman's italics.

56. Suleiman, "Nadja, Dora, Lol V. Stein," p. 146; my italics.

57. See, for instance, Brooks, "The Idea of a Psychoanalytic Literary Criticism," p. 336.

Chapter 2. *Gradiva:* Psychoanalysis as Archaeology

1. Jensen's *Gradiva* has been reprinted, together with Freud's reading, in *Der Wahn und die Träume in W. Jensen's 'Gradiva': Mit dem Text der Erzählung von Wilhelm Jensen*, ed. Bernd Urban and Johannes Cremerius (Frankfurt am Main: Fischer Taschenbuch Verlag, 1973). For an English translation of *Gradiva* see *Delusion and Dream: An Interpretation in the Light of Psychoanalysis of Gradiva, a Novel, by Wilhelm Jensen, Which Is Here Translated*, trans. Helen Downey (New York: Moffat, Yard and Co., 1917). Quotations from *Gradiva* are drawn from this translation which, unfortunately, differs from Strachey's translation of the passages cited in Freud's essay.

2. For two excellent readings of this essay see, however, Sarah Kofman, *Quatre romans analytiques*, and Mary Jacobus, "Is There a Woman in This Text?" *New Literary History* 14 (1982). Elizabeth Wright's summary of Freud's interpretation in *Psychoanalytic Criticism: Theory in Practice*, pp. 30–33, is brief but very much to the point.

3. *Delusions and Dreams in Jensen's* Gradiva (1907), *Standard Edition*, vol. IX, p. 7. Subsequent references to this work will be included in the main body of the text.

4. *Delusions and Dreams*, p. 91. See also *The Interpretation of Dreams, Standard Edition*, vol. IV, p. 97, n. 1 (added in 1909).

5. Sigmund Freud, *The Question of Lay Analysis* (1926), *Standard Edition*, vol. XX, p. 195.

6. Sigmund Freud, *Beyond the Pleasure Principle* (1920), *Standard Edition*, vol. XVIII, p. 60.

7. For critical discussions of Freud's analogy with archaeology see, for instance: Paul Ricoeur, *Freud and Philosophy: An Essay on Interpretation* (New Haven: Yale University Press, 1970); P. B. Jacobsen and R. S. Steele, "From Present to Past: Freudian Archaeology," *International Review of Psychoanalysis* 6 (1979); Serge Viderman, *La construction de l'espace analytique;* Donald P. Spence, *Narrative Truth and Historical Truth* and *The Freudian Metaphor;* Malcolm Bowie, *Freud, Proust and Lacan: Theory as Fiction.* Suzanne Bernfeld, in "Freud and Archaeology," *American Imago* 8 (1951) and Carl Schorske, in *Fin-de-Siècle Vienna* (New York: Vintage Books, 1981), read the analogy with archaeology in the context of Freud's relationship with his father and mother and of the cultural and political climate of the turn of the century. Finally, Walter Schönau,

Sigmund Freuds Prosa (Stuttgart: Metzler, 1968) includes Freud's analogy in his stylistic study of the literary elements of Freud's language.

8. Ricoeur, *Freud and Philosophy*, pp. 461, 420; Ricoeur's italics.

9. Editor's preface to "The Aetiology of Hysteria," p. 189.

10. "The Aetiology of Hysteria," p. 192.

11. Ricoeur, *Freud and Philosophy*, p. 433.

12. Sigmund Freud, *Notes upon a Case of Obsessional Neurosis* (1909), *Standard Edition*, vol. X, p. 176; Freud's italics.

13. Bernfeld, "Freud and Archaeology," p. 110. Ernest Jones gives the following description of Freud's consulting rooms in Vienna: "First there came a small waiting-room with a window giving on to the garden. . . . There was an oblong substantial table down the middle, and the room itself was decorated with various antiquities from Freud's collection. . . . The consulting room itself contained also many antiquities, including a relief of the famous Gradiva, and they no doubt afforded useful stimuli to patients' phantasies. It led into an inner sanctum, Freud's study proper. This was lined with books, but there was room for cabinets of still more antiquities. The desk at which he wrote was not large, but was always neat. To dust it must have been a trial, since it was replete with little statues, mostly Egyptian, which Freud used from time to time to replace by others from his cabinets" (*The Life and Work of Sigmund Freud*, vol. II [New York: Basic Books Inc., 1955], pp. 380–81). When Freud came to London in 1938 as a refugee from the Nazis, he brought his collection of antiquities. Freud's house in London is now a museum (the Freud Museum); the antiquity collection numbers over 2,500 artifacts.

14. *Letters of Sigmund Freud*, ed. Ernst Freud (New York: Basic Books, Inc., 1960), p. 403.

15. Schorske, *Fin-de-Siècle Vienna*, p. 189.

16. Bernfeld, "Freud and Archaeology," p. 111. "It has justly been said that 'every person of culture and education lived through the drama of discovering Troy,'" writes Glyn Daniel in *A Hundred and Fifty Years of Archaeology* (London: Duckworth, 1975), p. 138.

17. See H. Schliemann, *Troy and Its Remains: A Narrative of Researches and Discoveries Made on the Site of Ilium and in the Trojan Plain* (London: John Murray, 1875). Freud's library in the Freud Museum contains three books by Schliemann.

18. Sigmund Freud, *The Origins of Psychoanalysis: Letters to Wilhelm Fliess, Drafts and Notes 1887–1902*, ed. Marie Bonaparte, Anna Freud, and Ernst Kris (New York: Basic Books Inc., 1954), p. 333.

19. Evans's words are quoted from Ronald M. Burrows, *The Discoveries in Crete and Their Bearing on the History of Ancient Civilization* (London: John Murray, 1907), p. 2. The Freud Museum owns Freud's marked copy of this book.

20. Ibid., p. 204.

21. Schliemann, *Troy and Its Remains*, p. 80.

22. *The Origins of Psychoanalysis*, p. 305.

23. Brooks, *Reading for the Plot*, p. 6.

24. Daniel, *A Hundred and Fifty Years of Archaeology*, p. 165. Unfortunately, I cannot, within the scope of this book, go into a discussion of the history of archaeology or of the methodological and epistemological problems of archaeology. I am obliged to content myself with citing a few passages, drawn from

works on the history of archaeology, that may give an idea of how archaeology around the turn of the century conceived of its own objectives and methods.

25. Brooks, *Reading for the Plot,* p. 6.

26. "A hundred and fifty years ago the prehistory of mankind was *terra incognita,*" writes Geoffrey Bibby in *The Testimony of the Spade* (London: Collins, 1957), p. 428.

27. Massimo Pallottino, *The Meaning of Archaeology* (London: Thames and Hudson, 1968), p. 53.

28. *Studies on Hysteria,* p. 139.

29. "The Aetiology of Hysteria," p. 198.

30. Sigmund Freud, *Civilization and Its Discontents* (1930), *Standard Edition,* vol. XXI, p. 69.

31. *Delusions and Dreams in Jensen's Gradiva,* p. 40.

32. "Constructions in Analysis," p. 260.

33. Thomas de Quincey, "Suspiria de Profundis," in *Confessions of an English Opium Eater and Other Writings,* ed. Aileen Ward (New York: Carroll and Graf Publishers, 1985), p. 169. The Romantics' anticipation of psychoanalytic discoveries has been documented in Henri F. Ellenberger's massive study, *The Discovery of the Unconscious: The History and Evolution of Dynamic Psychiatry* (New York: Basic Books, 1970).

34. Jean Starobinski, "The Inside and the Outside," *The Hudson Review* 28, no. 3 (1975), p. 334.

35. Georges Poulet, "Timelessness and Romanticism," *Journal of the History of Ideas,* 15, no. 1 (1954), pp. 4, 11.

36. *Delusions and Dreams,* p. 40; *Studies on Hysteria,* p. 139.

37. In *The Subterfuge of Art: Language and the Romantic Tradition* (Baltimore: Johns Hopkins University Press, 1978), Michael Ragussis represents psychoanalysis as the culmination of the Romantic quest for "the earliest and most obscure moments of our past." Ragussis's study is itself an excellent example of the persistency of the analogy with archaeology in depth psychological thinking. "The child in Wordsworth's poetry and the savage in Keats's poetry suggest a grand march of intellect, to use Keats's phrase. There is first of all the march backwards to rediscover lost dreams and wishes. This is a regression for the simple dreamer, but an archaeology for the writer who uncovers what Freud calls the primeval period, the child and the savage in us" (p. 11). "Each literary work I will examine," Ragussis continues, "can be viewed as an archaeology, a cultural archaeology that discovers the beginnings of man" (p. 13). "One might say that what characterizes the movement of thought from Wordsworth, Hegel, and Keats, to Nietzsche, Freud, and Lawrence is a coherent search to appropriate a portion of the life history that has been lost. . . . Both writer and psychoanalyst, then, attempt to bring to light our prehistory" (p. 15).

38. Schafer, "Narration in the Psychoanalytic Dialogue," p. 26.

39. Ibid., p. 48.

40. Jacobsen and Steele, "From Present to Past: Freudian Archaeology," p. 351.

41. Habermas, *Knowledge and Human Interests,* p. 214.

42. "The Aetiology of Hysteria," p. 192; my italics.

43. *The Interpretation of Dreams,* vol. IV, p. 277.

44. Sigmund Freud, *The Claims of Psycho-Analysis to Scientific Interest* (1913), *Standard Edition,* vol. XIII, p. 177. In *Studies on Hysteria,* Freud makes use of the analogy with the bilingual inscription in order to illustrate how psychoanalysis

arrived at an understanding of the meaning of hysterical symptoms: "We . . . had often compared the symptomatology of hysteria with a pictographic script which has become intelligible after the discovery of a few bilingual inscriptions" (p. 129).

45. *The Interpretation of Dreams,* p. 97.

46. Sigmund Freud, *Introductory Lectures on Psycho-Analysis* (1916–17), *Standard Edition,* vol. XV, p. 229. Subsequent references are included in the text.

47. Spence, *The Freudian Metaphor,* p. 78.

48. Sigmund Freud, "Remarks on the Theory and Practice of Dream-Interpretation" (1923), *Standard Edition,* vol. XIX, p. 116.

49. See *Fragment of an Analysis of a Case of Hysteria,* p. 12.

50. Ricoeur, *Freud and Philosophy,* p. 433.

51. Spence, *The Freudian Metaphor,* p. 57.

52. *Gradiva,* in *Delusion and Dream: An Interpretation in the Light of Psychoanalysis of Gradiva, a Novel, by Wilhelm Jensen, Which Is Here Translated,* pp. 12–13.

53. Ibid., p. 108.

54. Ibid., p. 91.

55. Ibid., p. 98.

56. Jones, *The Life and Work of Sigmund Freud,* vol. 2, p. 342.

Chapter 3. Construction in the Case of the Wolf Man

1. Donald M. Kartiganer, "Freud's Reading Process: The Divided Protagonist Narrative and the Case of the Wolf-Man," in *The Psychoanalytic Study of Literature,* ed. J. Reppen and M. Charney (Hillsdale, N.J.: Analytical Press, 1985), p. 3.

2. Brooks, *Reading for the Plot,* p. 270.

3. Sigmund Freud, *From the History of an Infantile Neurosis* (1918), *Standard Edition,* vol. XVII, p. 54. Subsequent references will be included in the main body of the text.

4. Ned Lukacher, *Primal Scenes: Literature, Philosophy, Psychoanalysis* (Ithaca and London: Cornell University Press, 1986), p. 24.

5. It is from Freud's discussion, in this case, of the mechanism of *Verwerfung* (foreclosure, repudiation), as distinct from the mechanism of *Verdrängung* (repression) that Lacan derives his concept of *forclusion,* which is essential to his understanding of the structural differences between psychosis and neurosis. For Lacan's theory of foreclosure see "On a Question Preliminary to Any Possible Treatment of Psychosis" (1957–58). See also Lacan's discussion of the case of the Wolf Man in "The Function and Field of Speech and Language in Psychoanalysis" (1953). Both papers are reprinted in *Écrits: A Selection,* trans. Alan Sheridan (London: Tavistock, 1977). More recently, Nicolas Abraham and Maria Torok have offered a bold re-reading of Freud's analysis of the wolf dream. Taking into account the fact that the Wolf Man had at his disposal three different languages, Abraham and Torok suggest that he explored the phonetic similarities between Russian, English, and German words in order to relate his primal scene, which was, they argue, a scene of words: a conversation referring to an incestuous relationship between the father and the sister that the child had overheard. See *Cryptonomie: Le verbier de l'homme aux loups* (Paris: Aubier Flammarion, 1976).

6. See, for instance, Laplanche's essay, written in collaboration with J.-B. Pontalis, on "Fantasy and the Origins of Sexuality," *The International Journal of Psycho-Analysis* 49 (1968) and the chapter on deferred action, "Sexuality and the Vital Order in Psychical Conflict," in his own *Life and Death in Psychoanalysis*. Furthermore, I want to emphasize Brooks's excellent reading of the case of the Wolf Man in light of narrative theory in *Reading for the Plot,* pp. 264–85. See also Jonathan Culler's comments on *Nachträglichkeit* in *The Pursuit of Signs: Semiotics, Literature, Deconstruction* (London, Melbourne and Henley: Routledge and Kegan Paul, 1981), pp. 179–81.

7. The term "deferred action" is an insufficient or even misleading translation of the German term *Nachträglichkeit. Nachträglich* means "supplementary," "additional," "later," "subsequent." The German term thus emphasizes that something new, a supplement, is brought in.

8. See Brooks, *Reading for the Plot,* p. 277.

9. Sigmund Freud, "Analysis Terminable and Interminable" (1937), *Standard Edition,* vol. XXIII.

10. Sigmund Freud, "The Occurrence in Dreams of Material from Fairy Tales" (1913a), *Standard Edition,* vol. XII.

11. "Constructions in Analysis," p. 265.

12. "Remarks on the Theory and Practice of Dream-Interpretation," p. 115.

13. "Remembering, Repeating and Working-Through," p. 149.

14. Sigmund Freud, "Repression" (1915), *Standard Edition,* vol. XIV, p. 148.

15. Viderman, *La construction de l'espace analytique,* p. 17.

16. "The Aetiology of Hysteria," p. 193; Freud's italics.

17. Sigmund Freud, *Introductory Lectures on Psycho-Analysis* (1916–17), *Standard Edition,* vol. XVI, p. 368; Freud's italics.

18. In *Introductory Lectures on Psycho-Analysis,* which was written in the years between the writing and the publication of *From the History of an Infantile Neurosis,* Freud states that recollections of parental coitus a tergo as a rule must be regarded as fantasies rather than as memories of real events: "If . . . the intercourse is described with the most minute details, which would be difficult to observe, or if, as it happens most frequently, it turns out to be an intercourse from behind, *more ferarum* [in the manner of animals], there can be no remaining doubt that the phantasy is based on an observation of intercourse between animals (such as dogs)" (p. 369).

19. Ibid., p. 368.

20. Culler, *The Pursuit of Signs,* p. 181.

21. Brooks, *Reading for the Plot,* p. 275.

22. *Introductory Lectures,* p. 371; Freud's italics.

23. Laplanche and Pontalis, "Fantasy and the Origins of Sexuality," pp. 9–10.

24. "The Aetiology of Hysteria," pp. 202, 213; Freud's italics. Jeffrey Moussaieff Masson has recently suggested that Freud abandoned—indeed, *suppressed*—the seduction theory for personal rather than for clinical or theoretical reasons. "The Aetiology of Hysteria," he claims, launched the theory that the origin of neurosis lay in early experiences of sexual abuse. It was this theory that Freud later abandoned out of lack of courage. Significantly, Masson's paraphrase of "The Aetiology of Hysteria" suppresses Freud's discussion of the role played by memory in the formation of neurosis. In so doing, he

misrepresents Freud's argument. See Masson's *Freud: The Assault on Truth. Freud's Suppression of the Seduction Theory* (London and Boston: Faber and Faber, 1984).

25. Sigmund Freud, *Project for a Scientific Psychology* (1950b), *Standard Edition*, vol. 1, p. 354. Subsequent references to the analysis of Emma are included in the text.

26. Laplanche, *Life and Death in Psychoanalysis*, pp. 41–42; my italics.

27. Ibid., p. 40; Laplanche's italics.

28. Sigmund Freud, *Extracts from the Fliess Papers*, p. 233; Freud's italics.

29. "Constructions in Analysis," p. 262.

30. Lukacher, *Primal Scenes*, p. 149.

31. "Constructions in Analysis," p. 263.

32. Ibid., p. 259.

33. *Fragment of an Analysis of a Case of Hysteria*, p. 12.

34. *Moses and Monotheism*, p. 130; Freud's italics.

35. "Remarks on the Theory and Practice of Dream-Interpretation," p. 115.

36. This understanding of the dream work is consistent with a footnote in *The Interpretation of Dreams*, added in 1925: "They [the analysts] seek to find the essence of dreams in their latent content and in so doing they overlook the distinction between the latent dream-thoughts and the dream-work. At bottom, dreams are nothing other than a particular *form* of thinking, made possible by the conditions of the state of sleep. It is the *dream-work* which creates that form, and it alone is the essence of dreaming—the explanation of its peculiar nature" (*The Interpretation of Dreams, Standard Edition*, vol. V, p. 506, n. 2).

37. Spence, *Narrative Truth and Historical Truth*, p. 117.

38. Jakobsen and Steele, "From Present to Past: Freudian Archaeology," p. 356.

39. Brooks, *Reading for the Plot*, p. 283.

40. Kartiganer, "Freud's Reading Process," p. 32. Later in his life, however, the Wolf Man referred to the constructed scene as "terribly far-fetched" and appointed the sister's seduction as primal scene. For a discussion of the Wolf Man's abandonment of the analytical construction see Lukacher, *Primal Scenes*, pp. 136–67.

41. Brooks, *Reading for the Plot*, p. 283.

Chapter 4. *Gradiva:* Textual Archaeology and the Ghost of Fiction

1. Sigmund Freud, "Postscript to the Second Edition" (1912), *Standard Edition*, vol. IX, p. 94.

2. Kofman, *Quatre romans analytiques*, p. 125.

3. *Delusions and Dreams in Jensen's* Gradiva, p. 40. Subsequent references to this work will be included in the text.

4. Wilhelm Jensen, *Gradiva*, in *Delusion and Dream. An Interpretation in the Light of Psychoanalysis* of Gradiva, *a Novel, by Wilhelm Jensen, Which Is Here Translated*, pp. 22–23.

5. Ibid., p. 25.

6. See Baudry, "Freud et 'la crétion littéraire.'"

7. Skura, *The Literary Use of the Psychoanalytic Process*, p. 48.

8. Jacobus, "Is There a Woman in This Text?" p. 124.

9. Kofman, *Quatre romans analytiques*, p. 102. According to Kofman, the

summary turns out to be a "supplement dangereux." Does not the analyst, she asks, in his attempt to extract the substance of the story, create a new text?

10. Rieff, *Freud: The Mind of the Moralist,* pp. 120, 121.

11. Sigmund Freud, "The Moses of Michelangelo" (1914a), *Standard Edition,* vol. XIII, pp. 211, 212; Freud's italics.

12. Sigmund Freud, *Jokes and Their Relation to the Unconscious* (1905a), *Standard Edition,* vol. VIII, pp. 96, 103, 136–37; Freud's italics. It should be noted that my brief summary does not do justice to this rich and complex text. As it turns out, Freud ends by deconstructing the hierarchical relationship between "technique" and "thought" that I have outlined. For an excellent reading of *Jokes and Their Relation to the Unconscious* see Samuel Weber, *Freud-Legende,* pp. 111–43.

13. Sigmund Freud, "Creative Writers and Day-Dreaming" (1908), *Standard Edition,* vol. IX, p. 153; Freud's italics.

14. "Postscript to the Second Edition," pp. 94, 95.

15. Quoted from Jones, *The Life and Work of Sigmund Freud,* vol. 2, p. 343. Freud presented this hypothesis before the Vienna Society (December 1907).

16. "Creative Writers and Day-Dreaming," pp. 146, 151.

17. *Introductory Lectures on Psycho-Analysis, Standard Edition,* vol. XVI, p. 376.

18. Ibid.

19. "Creative Writers and Day-Dreaming," p. 153.

20. *Introductory Lectures,* p. 376.

21. Freud made this observation in a letter to Jung (May 26, 1907). *Letters of Sigmund Freud,* pp. 252–53.

22. Chabot, *Freud on Schreber,* p. 70.

23. "Remarks on the Theory and Practice of Dream-Interpretation," p. 116.

24. Rieff, *Freud: The Mind of a Moralist,* p. 115.

25. Ricoeur, *Freud and Philosophy,* p. 433.

26. Ibid.

27. Rieff, *Freud: The Mind of the Moralist,* p. 117.

28. In her essay "Is There a Woman in this Text?" Mary Jacobus discusses Freud's attempt to account for the similarity between Zoe and the relief. I am indebted to Jacobus's article for having called attention to the peculiarity of Freud's construction. Her reading of this construction is, however, different from my own. Freud gives "priority to the representation over what it represents," she writes. "This peculiarity exactly parallels the priority of Freudian theory over the literary text. As Gradiva is to Zoe, so is theory to Jensen's novella" (p. 124).

29. *Gradiva,* p. 11.

30. Ibid., p. 14.

31. "Postscript to the Second Edition," p. 94.

Chapter 5. "The Sandman": The Uncanny as Problem of Reading

1. "The Uncanny" (1919), *Standard Edition,* vol. XVII, p. 232, n. 1; my italics. Subsequent references will be included in the text.

2. Hélène Cixous, "Fiction and Its Phantoms: A Reading of Freud's *Das Unheimliche* (The Uncanny)," *New Literary History* 7, no. 3 (1976), p. 537.

Cixous's article is only one of several interesting readings of Freud's essay (see note 4).

3. Crews, *Out of My System,* p. xiii.

4. See Sarah Kofman's reading, "Le double e(s)t le diable," in *Quatre romans analytique.* "The Uncanny" (and, in particular, Freud's interpretation of "The Sandman") has been the occasion for a number of brilliant poststructuralist and deconstructive readings. In addition to those listed above, I would like to mention the following: Samuel Weber, "The Sideshow, or: Remarks on a Canny Moment," *MLN* 88, no. 6 (1973), 1102–33; Jeffrey Mehlman, "Poe Pourri: Lacan's Purloined Letter," *Semiotext(e)* 1 (1975), 51–68; Neil Hertz, "Freud and the Sandman" in *Textual Strategies,* ed. J. Harari (Ithaca, N.Y.: Cornell University Press, 1979). I shall refer to these works in the following. For an excellent outline and discussion of different poststructuralist readings of "The Uncanny," see Elizabeth Wright, *Psychoanalytic Criticism: Theory in Practice,* pp. 142–50. See also Meredith Anne Skura, *The Literary Use of the Psychoanalytic Process,* pp. 216–22.

5. Freud's reading of "The Sandman" demonstrates "les impasses d'une lecture thématique" of the uncanny, Kofman contends; "il devient impossible de conclure l'effet à partir du thème" (p. 146).

6. A third variant of Freud's treatment of this literary theme is to be found in "The Theme of the Three Caskets" (1917) (*Standard Edition,* vol. XII). In this essay, Freud draws a parallel between Bassanio's choice of the lead casket (*The Merchant of Venice*) and King Lear's final choice of the silent Cordelia (*King Lear*), arguing that these choices represent man's choice of the woman who signifies Death.

7. "The Sandman," p. 111. Quotations from Hoffmann's narrative are taken from *Tales from Hoffmann,* ed. J. M. Cohen (New York: Conard-Mc.Cann Inc., 1951). Subsequent references are included in the main body of the text.

8. Hertz, "Freud and the Sandman," p. 304.

9. Kofman, *Quatre romans analytiques,* p. 161. The (torn-out) eye, Kofman argues, is thus, quite literally, a substitute for the sexual organ: "Si l'oeil, dans la nouvelle, est bien un substitut du sexe, il faut entendre cette expression à la lettre et non symboliquement" (p. 161).

10. Freud's refutation of Jentsch's theory and the return of the issue of "uncertainty" in "The Uncanny" have been discussed by Kofman, as well as by Weber and Cixous. "Does not Jentsch say more than Freud wishes to read?" asks Cixous ("Fiction and Its Phantoms," p. 534), who, in accordance with Kofman and Weber, goes on to suggest that the uncanny effect is inextricably bound up with uncertainty. In the following, I shall expose the shifts and displacements within Freud's argument that ultimately will lead him to a very similar conclusion.

11. Tzvetan Todorov, *The Poetics of Prose* (Oxford: Basil Blackwell, 1977) p. 179.

12. James Strachey, the editor of *The Standard Edition,* has contributed to this negligence by referring the reader to J. M. Cohen's translation of "Der Sandmann" in *Eight Tales of Hoffmann* (London: Pan Books, 1952). This edition has left out the important passage in which the narrator, addressing the reader, testifies to his difficulties in telling the story. "I have taken the liberty," writes Cohen in his introduction, "of removing a page of rambling rumination which holds up the development of 'The Sandman'" (p. 13).

13. "The Uncanny" opens with a remarkable etymological investigation

of the terms *heimlich* and *unheimlich* that demonstrates that "among its different shades of meaning the word *'heimlich'* exhibits one which is identical with its opposite, *'unheimlich.'* What is *heimlich* thus comes to be *unheimlch*" (p. 224). On the one hand *heimlich* means that which is familiar, intimate, not strange; on the other hand, it means that which is concealed and kept out of sight. The word *unheimlich* proceeds from this second meaning of *heimlich*. In Grimm's dictionary: *"The notion of something hidden and dangerous . . . is still further developed, so that 'heimlich' comes to have a meaning usually ascribed to 'unheimlich'"* (p. 226; Freud's italics). "Thus *heimlich*," writes Freud, "is a word the meaning of which develops in the direction of ambivalence, until it finally coincides with its opposite, *unheimlich*" (p. 226).

14. "The Sandman," p. 11.

15. *Beyond the Pleasure Principle,* pp. 35–36; Freud's italics.

16. This is Cixous's point. It is not merely the question of examining the enigma of the uncanny, she says, but also of examining the enigma of fiction, "and of fiction in its privileged relationship to the *Unheimliche*" (p. 546).

Works Cited

Abraham, Nicolas. "The Shell and the Kernel." *Diacritics* (March 1979):16–28.

Abraham, Nicolas, and Maria Torok. *Cryptonomie: Le verbier de l'homme aux loups*. Paris: Aubier Flammarion, 1976.

Adorno, Theodor Wiesengrund. *Ästhetische Theorie*. Frankfurt am Main: Suhrkamp, 1970.

Baudry, Jean-Louis. "Freud et 'la création littéraire.'" *Tel Quel* 32 (1968):63–85.

Bernfeld, Suzanne Cassirer. "Freud and Archaeology." *American Imago* 8 (1951):107–28.

Bernheimer, Charles, and Claire Kahane, eds. *In Dora's Case: Freud—Hysteria—Feminism*. New York: Columbia University Press, 1985.

Bibby, Geoffrey. *The Testimony of the Spade*. London: Collins, 1957.

Bowie, Malcolm. *Freud, Proust and Lacan: Theory as Fiction*. Cambridge: Cambridge University Press, 1987.

Brooks, Peter. "Constructions psychanalytiques et narratives." *Poétique* 61 (1985):63–74.

———. *Reading for the Plot: Design and Intention in Narrative*. New York: Vintage Books, 1985.

———. "Psychoanalytic Constructions and Narrative Meanings." *Paragraph* (1986):53–76.

———. "The Idea of a Psychoanalytic Literary Criticism." *Critical Inquiry* 13 (1987):334–48.

Burrows, Ronald M. *The Discoveries in Crete and Their Bearing on the History of Ancient Civilization*. London: John Murray, 1907.

Cardinal, Maria. *Les mots pour le dire*. Paris: Bernard Grasset, 1975.

Chabot, C. Barry. *Freud on Schreber: Psychoanalytic Theory and the Critical Act*. Amherst: University of Massachusetts Press, 1982.

Cixous, Hélène. "Fiction and Its Phantoms: A Reading of Freud's *Das Unheimliche* (The Uncanny)." *New Literary History* 7 (1976):525–48.

Crews, Frederick. *The Sins of the Fathers: Hawthorne's Psychological Themes*. New York: Oxford University Press, 1966.

———. *Out of My System: Psychoanalysis, Ideology, and Critical Method*. New York: Oxford University Press, 1975.

Culler, Jonathan. *The Pursuit of Signs: Semiotics, Literature, Deconstruction*. London, Melbourne and Henley: Routledge and Kegan Paul, 1981.

Dalton, Elizabeth. *Unconscious Structure in* The Idiot: *A Study in Literature and Psychoanalysis*. Princeton: Princeton University Press, 1979.

Daniel, Glyn. *A Hundred and Fifty Years of Archaeology.* London: Duckworth, 1975.

de Quincey, Thomas. "Suspiria de Profundis." In *Confessions of an English Opium Eater and Other Writings,* ed. Aileen Ward. New York: Carroll and Graf Publishers, 1985.

Ellenberger, Henri F. *The Discovery of the Unconscious: The History and Evolution of Dynamic Psychiatry.* New York: Basic Books, 1970.

Felman, Shoshana. "To Open the Question." *Literature and Psychoanalysis: The Question of Reading: Otherwise,* ed. Shoshana Felman. Baltimore and London: Johns Hopkins University Press, 1982.

———. "Turning the Screw of Interpretation." In *Literature and Psychoanalysis: The Question of Reading: Otherwise,* ed. Shoshana Felman. Baltimore and London: Johns Hopkins University Press, 1982.

———. "On Reading Poetry: Reflections on the Limits and Possibilities of Psychoanalytic Approaches." In *The Purloined Poe: Lacan, Derrida, and Psychoanalytic Reading,* ed. John P. Muller and William J. Richardson. Baltimore and London: Johns Hopkins University Press, 1988.

Freud, Sigmund (in collaboration with Josef Breuer). 1895. *Studies on Hysteria.* Vol. II of *The Standard Edition of the Complete Psychological Works of Sigmund Freud.* Translated from the German under the general editorship of James Strachey, in collaboration with Anna Freud, assisted by Alix Strachey and Alan Tyson. 24 vols. London: Hogarth Press, 1953–1974.

———. 1896a. "Further Remarks on the Neuro-Psychoses of Defense." In *The Standard Edition,* vol. III.

———. 1896b. "The Aetiology of Hysteria." In *The Standard Edition,* vol. III.

———. 1899. "Screen Memories." In *The Standard Edition,* vol. III.

———. 1900. *The Interpretation of Dreams.* In *The Standard Edition,* vols. IV–V.

———. 1905a. *Jokes and Their Relation to the Unconscious.* In *The Standard Edition,* vol. VIII.

———. 1905b. *Fragment of an Analysis of a Case of Hysteria.* In *The Standard Edition,* vol. VII.

———. 1907. *Delusions and Dreams in Jensen's Gradiva.* In *The Standard Edition,* vol. IX.

———. 1908. "Creative Writers and Day-Dreaming." In *The Standard Edition,* vol. IX.

———. 1909. "Notes upon a Case of Obsessional Neurosis." In *The Standard Edition,* vol. X.

———. 1910. *Leonardo da Vinci and a Memory of His Childhood.* In *The Standard Edition,* vol. XI.

———. 1913a. "The Occurrence in Dreams of Material from Fairy Tales." In *The Standard Edition,* vol. XII.

———. 1913b. "The Claims of Psycho-Analysis to Scientific Interest." In *The Standard Edition,* vol. XIII.

———. 1914a. "The Moses of Michelangelo." In *The Standard Edition,* vol. XIII.

———. 1914b. "Remembering, Repeating and Working-Through." In *The Standard Edition,* vol. XII.

———. 1915. "Repression." In *The Standard Edition,* vol. XIV.

———. 1916–17. *Introductory Lectures on Psycho-Analysis.* In *The Standard Edition,* vols. XV–XVI.

———. 1917. "The Theme of the Three Caskets." In *The Standard Edition,* vol. XII.

————. 1918. *From the History of an Infantile Neurosis.* In *The Standard Edition,* vol. XVII.

————. 1919. "The Uncanny." In *The Standard Edition,* vol. XVII.

————. 1920. *Beyond the Pleasure Principle.* In *The Standard Edition,* vol. XVIII.

————. 1923. "Remarks on the Theory and Practice of Dream-Interpretation." In *The Standard Edition,* vol. XIX.

————. 1926. *The Question of Lay Analysis.* In *The Standard Edition,* vol. XX.

————. 1930. *Civilization and Its Discontents.* In *The Standard Edition,* vol. XXI.

————. 1937a. "Analysis Terminable and Interminable." In *The Standard Edition,* vol. XXIII.

————. 1937b. "Constructions in Analysis." In *The Standard Edition,* vol. XXIII.

————. 1939. *Moses and Monotheism.* In *The Standard Edition,* vol. XXIII.

————. 1950a. *Extracts from the Fliess Papers.* In *The Standard Edition,* vol. I.

————. 1950b. *Project for a Scientific Psychology.* In *The Standard Edition,* vol. I.

————. 1954. *The Origins of Psychoanalysis. Letters to Wilhelm Fliess, Drafts and Notes 1887–1902.* Ed. Marie Bonaparte, Anna Freud, and Ernst Kris. New York: Basic Books Inc., 1954.

————. 1960. *Letters of Sigmund Freud.* Ed. Ernst Freud. New York: Basic Books, Inc., 1960.

Green, André. "The Analyst, Symbolization, and Absence in the Analytical Setting." *International Journal of Psycho-Analysis* 56 (1975):1–22.

Habermas, Jürgen. *Knowledge and Human Interests.* Trans. Jeremy J. Shapiro. Boston: Beacon Press, 1971.

Hertz, Neil. "Freud and the Sandman." In *Textual Strategies,* ed. J. Harari. Ithaca, N.Y.: Cornell University Press, 1979.

Hoffmann, E. T. A. "The Sandman." *Tales from Hoffmann.* Trans. by various hands, ed. J. M. Cohen. New York: Conard-Mc.Cann Inc., 1951.

————. *Eight Tales of Hoffmann.* Trans. J. M. Cohen. London: Pan Books, 1952.

Jacobsen, P. B., and R. S. Steele. "From Present to Past: Freudian Archaeology." *International Review of Psychoanalysis* 6 (1979):349–62.

Jacobus, Mary. "Is There a Woman in This Text?" *New Literary History* 14 (1982):117–41.

Jay, Paul. *Being in the Text. Self-Representation from Wordsworth to Roland Barthes.* Ithaca and London: Cornell University Press, 1984.

Jensen, Wilhelm. *Gradiva.* In *Delusion and Dream. An Interpretation in the Light of Psychoanalysis* of Gradiva, *a Novel, by Wilhelm Jensen, Which Is Here Translated.* Trans. Helen Downey. New York: Moffat, Yard and Co., 1917.

————. *Gradiva. Ein pompejanisches Phantasiestück.* In *Der Wahn und die Träume in W. Jensens 'Gradiva'. Mit dem Text der Erzählung von Wilhelm Jensen,* ed. Bernd Urban and Johannes Cremerius. Frankfurt am Main: Fischer Taschenbuch Verlag, 1973.

Jones, Ernest. *The Life and Work of Sigmund Freud.* 3 vols. New York: Basic Books, 1953–57.

————. *Hamlet and Oedipus.* New York: W.W. Norton and Company, 1976.

Kartiganer, Donald M. "Freud's Reading Process: The Divided Protagonist Narrative and the Case of the Wolf-Man." In *The Psychoanalytic Study of Literature,* ed. J. Reppen and M. Charney. Hillsdale, N.J.: Analytical Press, 1985.

Kofman, Sarah. *L'enfance de l'art: Une interprétation de l'esthétique freudienne.* Paris: Payot, 1970.

————. *Quatre romans analytiques.* Paris: Galilée, 1973.

Kristeva, Julia. "Psychoanalysis and the Polis." In *The Politics of Interpretation,* ed. W. J. T. Mitchell. Chicago and London: University of Chicago Press, 1983.

Lacan, Jacques. *Écrits: A Selection.* Trans. Alan Sheridan. London: Tavistock, 1977.

———. "Intervention on Transference." In *In Dora's Case,* ed. Charles Bernheimer and Claire Kahane. New York: Columbia University Press, 1985.

Laplanche, Jean. *Life and Death in Psychoanalysis.* Trans. Jeffrey Mehlman. Baltimore and London: Johns Hopkins University Press, 1976.

Laplanche, Jean, and J.-B. Pontalis. "Fantasy and the Origins of Sexuality." *International Journal of Psycho-Analysis* 49 (1968):1–18.

Lesser, Simon O. *Fiction and the Unconscious.* Boston: Beacon Press, 1957.

Loch, Wolfgang. "Psychoanalysis and Truth." In *Thought, Consciousness and Reality,* ed. J. H. Smith. *Psychiatry and the Humanities.* Vol. II. New Haven: Yale University Press, 1977.

Lukacher, Ned. *Primal Scenes: Literature, Philosophy, Psychoanalysis.* Ithaca and London: Cornell University Press, 1986.

Marcus, Steven. *Freud and the Culture of Psychoanalysis.* New York and London: W.W. Norton and Company, 1987.

Masson, Jeffrey Moussaieff. *Freud: The Assault on Truth. Freud's Suppression of the Seduction Theory.* London and Boston: Faber and Faber, 1984.

Mehlman, Jeffrey. "Poe Pourri: Lacan's Purloined Letter." *Semiotext(e)* 1 (1975): 51–68.

Meisel, Perry. "Introduction: Freud as Literature." In *Freud: A Collection of Critical Essays,* ed. Perry Meisel. Englewood Cliffs, N.J.: Prentice-Hall, 1981.

Moi, Toril. "Representation of Patriarchy: Sexuality and Epistemology in Freud's Dora." In *In Dora's Case. Freud—Hysteria—Feminism,* ed. Charles Bernheimer and Claire Kahane. New York: Columbia University Press, 1985.

Pallottino, Massimo. *The Meaning of Archaeology.* London: Thames and Hudson, 1968.

Poulet, Georges. "Timelessness and Romanticism." *Journal of the History of Ideas* 15 (January 1954):3–22.

Ragussis, Michael. *The Subterfuge of Art: Language and the Romantic Tradition.* Baltimore: Johns Hopkins University Press, 1978.

Ricoeur, Paul. *Freud and Philosophy: An Essay on Interpretation.* New Haven: Yale University Press, 1970.

Rieff, Philip. *Freud: The Mind of the Moralist.* 3d ed. Chicago and London: University of Chicago Press, 1979.

Schafer, Roy. "Narration in the Psychoanalytic Dialogue." In *On Narrative,* ed. W. J. T. Mitchell. Chicago and London: University of Chicago Press, 1981.

Schliemann, Heinrich. *Troy and Its Remains: A Narrative of Researches and Discoveries Made on the Site of Ilium and in the Trojan Plain.* London: John Murray, 1875.

Schönau, Walter. *Sigmund Freuds Prosa.* Stuttgart: Metzler, 1968.

Schorske, Carl. *Fin-de-Siècle Vienna.* New York: Vintage Books, 1981.

Skura, Meredith Anne. *The Literary Use of the Psychoanalytic Process.* New Haven and London: Yale University Press, 1981.

Spence, Donald P. *Narrative Truth and Historical Truth: Meaning and Interpretation in Psychoanalysis.* New York and London: W.W. Norton and Company, 1982.

————. *The Freudian Metaphor: Toward Paradigm Change in Psychoanalysis*. New York and London: W.W. Norton and Company, 1987.

Starobinski, Jean. "The Inside and the Outside." *The Hudson Review* 28 (1975): 333–51.

Suleiman, Susan Rubin. "Nadja, Dora, Lol V. Stein: Women, Madness and Narrative." In *Discourse in Psychoanalysis and Literature*, ed. Shlomith Rimmon-Kenan. London and New York: Methuen, 1987.

Todorov, Tzvetan. *The Poetics of Prose*. Oxford: Basil Blackwell, 1977.

Trilling, Lionel. "Freud and Literature." In *Freud: A Collection of Critical Essays*, ed. Perry Meisel. Englewood Cliffs, N.J.: Prentice-Hall, 1981.

Viderman, Serge. *La construction de l'espace analytique*. Paris: Gallimard, 1982.

Weber, Samuel. "The Sideshow, or: Remarks on a Canny Moment." *MLN* 88 no. 6 (1973):1102–33.

————. *Freud-Legende*. Olten und Freiburg: Walter-Verlag, 1979.

White, Hayden. "Historical Pluralism." *Critical Inquiry* 12 (1986):480–93.

Wright, Elizabeth. *Psychoanalytic Criticism: Theory in Practice*. London and New York: Methuen, 1984.

Index

This book was set in Baskerville and Eras typefaces. Baskerville was designed by John Baskerville at his private press in Birmingham, England, in the eighteenth century. The first typeface to depart from oldstyle typeface design, Baskerville has more variation between thick and thin strokes. In an effort to insure that the thick and thin strokes of his typeface reproduced well on paper, John Baskerville developed the first wove paper, the surface of which was much smoother than the laid paper of the time. The development of wove paper was partly responsible for the introduction of typefaces classified as modern, which have even more contrast between thick and thin strokes.

Eras was designed in 1969 by Studio Hollenstein in Paris for the Wagner Typefoundry. A contemporary script-like version of a sans-serif typeface, the letters of Eras have a monotone stroke and are slightly inclined.

Printed on acid-free paper.